Knit a
NURSERY
RHYME

BELINDA RUSHWORTH-LUND

BLOOMSBURY

To Crispin, Louis and Alice

This edition first published 1989
Bloomsbury Publishing Limited
2 Soho Square
London W1V 5DE

Designed and produced by Rosemary Wilkinson,
30 Blackroot Road, Sutton Coldfield, B74 2QP

Design and illustrations © 1989 Rosemary Wilkinson
Text and pattern designs © 1989 Belinda Rushworth-Lund

Designer: Frances de Rees
Photographer: Pablo Keller
Illustrators: Marilyn Clark; Belinda Rushworth-Lund

With thanks to the following:

The models: Lee Benney; Alice Rushworth-Lund; Louis
Rushworth-Lund; Darcy van Hinsberg; Louis van
Hinsberg; Harriet Winfrey

The knitters: Hilary Evison; Sally Goodwin; Jerry Lewis;
Dorothy Wilkinson

And special thanks to parents Jock & Hazel Williamson for
looking after Louis & Alice while I was working on the
designs.

The text for the nursery rhymes is reproduced by kind
permission of Oxford University Press from the 'Oxford
Nursery Rhyme Book', assembled by Iona and Peter Opie
(1955).

CIP catalogue record for this book is available from the
British Library

ISBN 0–7475–0469–5

Typeset by Fakenham Photosetting Ltd, Fakenham,
Norfolk
Printed in Belgium

Contents

*H*umpty Dumpty sat on a wall,
Humpty Dumpty had a great fall;
All the King's horses and all the King's men
Couldn't put Humpty together again.

Humpty Dumpty

Humpty Dumpty before his fall is shown on this chunky winter jumper for boys or girls. Matching hat and socks complete the outfit. Humpty Dumpty also makes a nice round cuddly toy with his own egg cosy tucked into his pocket.

MEASUREMENTS

Jumper
Chest: 51 (56, 61) cm / 20 (22, 24) in
Length from centre back of neck: 34 (37, 39) cm / 13½ (14½, 15½) in
Sleeve: 22 (24, 27) cm / 8½ (9½, 10½) in

Hat (one size)
Width round head: 42 cm / 16½ in

Socks
One size: 1–4 years

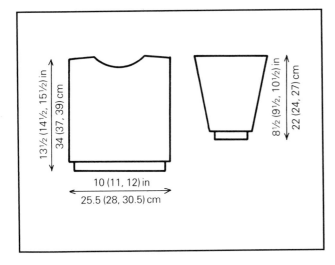

MATERIALS

Wool
The numbers in brackets after the colours refer to Rowan Yarns chunky for the jumper and DK lightweight for the socks and hat. Any other chunky or double knitting can be used provided the tension is the same.

	Jumper	Hat	Socks
Nelson blue (723) [MS]	125 g (175 g, 225 g)		
hunting pink (114)	50 g		
viola (722)	50 g (75 g, 100g)		
yellow (DK 13) – used double)	25 g		
natural (35)	25 g		
red (42)		50 g	50 g

Alternative colourway
Use nautilus (727), a turquoise tweed, in place of the nelson blue.

Needles and notions
1 pair 6 mm (no. 4), 1 pair 7 mm (no. 2), 1 pair 3¼ mm (no. 10) and 1 pair 4 mm (no. 8) needles; 3 buttons (for fastening jumper); 5 buttons (to sew on Humpty Dumpty); ribbon for bow tie

TENSION

14 sts. × 18 rows st.st. on 7 mm (no. 2) needles makes a 10 cm / 4 in square

PATTERN

JUMPER

Back
Using 6 mm (no. 4) needles and red, cast on 39 (41, 45) sts.
Work in k1, p1, rib for 2.5 cm / 1 in.
Inc. 1 st. at end of next rib row. *40 (42, 46) sts.*
Change to 7 mm (no. 2) needles.
** Following the chart on page 8 and starting at line 1, cont. on these sts. until work measures 28 (33, 37.5) cm / 11 (13,

14¾) in and working in st.st. except for the wall section of the chart which is worked in brick patt.

Note: For a simpler version, the wall can be worked in st.st. as the rest of the jumper.

Work brick patt. as follows:

Brick st.
1st row: k2, p2, to end of row.
2nd row: p2, k2, to end of row.
3rd row: p2, k2, to end of row.
4th row: k2, p2, to end of row.
These 4 rows form the pattern.
Rep. last 4 rows 3 times (16 rows) as indicated on chart.

Shape left shoulder
Next row: knit to last 12 (12, 13) sts., cast off these sts. Break off yarn, turn, rejoin yarn to rem. sts.
Next row: purl.

Shape right shoulder
Cast off 12 (12, 13) sts., knit to end.
Slip rem. 16 (18, 20) sts. onto a stitch holder. Break off yarn.

Front
Following chart for front on page 8, work as for back until work measures 7 rows shorter than back before shaping shoulder.

Shape neck
Next row: p 25 (p26, p28), slip last 10 sts. just worked onto a stitch holder, purl to end.
Cont. on last set of sts. as follows:
Dec. 1 st. at neck edge on every row until 12 (12, 13) sts. remain.
Work 3 (2, 3) rows.

Shape shoulder
Cast off. With right side facing, rejoin yarn to rem sts. at neck edge.
Dec. 1 st. at neck edge on every row until 12 (12, 13) sts. remain.
Work a further 5 (4, 5) rows. Cast off.

Sleeves
Using 6 mm (no. 4) needles and purple, cast on 21 (23, 25) sts. Work 2.5 cm / 1 in rib as back, increasing 1 st. at end of last row. *22 (24, 26) sts.*
Change to 7 mm (no. 2) needles.
Cont. in st.st. following the chart for the sleeve below, increasing 1 st. at each end of needle on the 3rd and every following 4 (4, 6) rows until 32 (28, 34) sts. rem.
56 (61) cm / 22 (24) in sizes only: inc. 1 st. at each end of needle on every following 6 (8) rows until 36 (38) sts. remain.
All sizes: Work a further 9 (9, 11) rows. *Work should measure 18.5 (25.5, 29) cm / 7¼ (10, 11½) in from beg.*
Cast off loosely.

Make up
Join right shoulder seam.

Neckband
With right side facing, using 6 mm (no. 4) needles and blue, pick up 8 (8, 10) sts. down left side neck, knit 10 sts. from front neck stitch holder, pick up and knit 9 (9, 11) sts. up right side neck and knit 16 (18, 20) sts. from back neck stitch holder. *43 (45, 51) sts.*
Cont. in rib for 7.5 (9, 9) cm / 3 (3½, 3½) in.
Cast off loosely in rib.
Fold neckband in half onto WS and slip stitch into position.

Front shoulder buttonhole band
With right side facing, using 6 mm (no. 4) needles and blue, start at armhole edge and pick up and knit 17 (18, 19) sts. along left shoulder and up neckband, taking in both thicknesses of neckband.
Next row: * p1, k1, rep. from * to last 1 (0, 1) sts., p1 (p0, p1).
Next row: (buttonhole row): rib 2 (3, 2) sts., * yrn to make a st., rib 2 tog., rib 4 (4, 5) sts., rep. from * once more, yrn to make a st., rib 2 tog., rib 1.
Work 1 more rib row. Cast off in rib.

Back shoulder buttonband
With right side facing, using 6 mm (no. 4) needles and blue, start at top of neckband, pick up and knit 17 (18, 19) sts. down

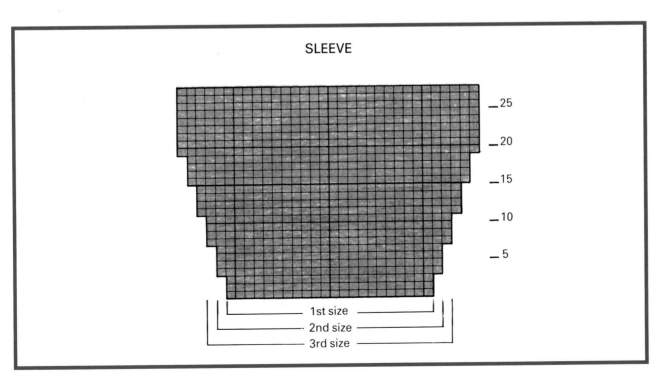

SLEEVE

—25
—20
—15
—10
—5

1st size
2nd size
3rd size

FRONT
Embroider eyebrows in loop st.

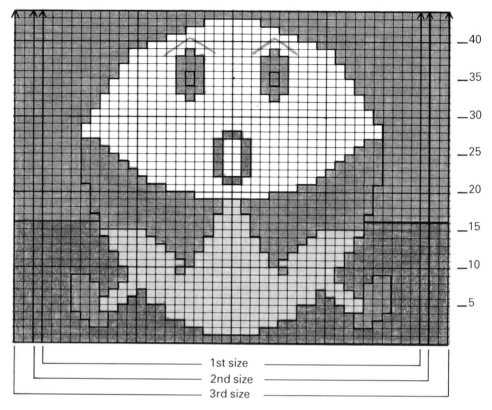

—40
—35
—30
—25
—20
—15
—10
—5

1st size
2nd size
3rd size

Wall in brick pattern

BACK

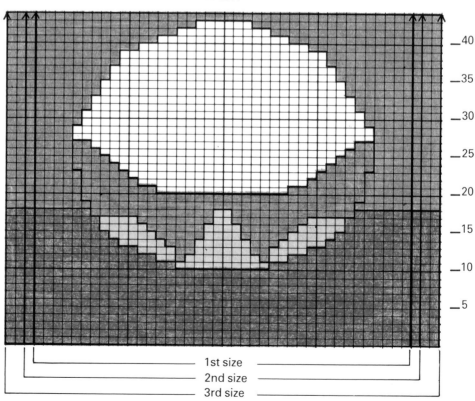

—40
—35
—30
—25
—20
—15
—10
—5

1st size
2nd size
3rd size

neckband and along shoulder edge, taking in both thicknesses of neckband.
Next row: p1 (p0, p1), * k1, p1, rep. from * to end.
Work 2 rows rib.
Cast off in rib.
Place buttonhole band over buttonband and slip stitch together at armhole edge. Mark depth of armholes 11.5 (12.5, 14) cm /4½ (5, 5½)in from shoulder. Join side seams to markers and sleeve seams. Put sleeves in position and sew on. Lightly press all seams on wrong side. Sew buttons on shoulder at back to correspond to buttonholes. Make a bow tie out of ribbon and stitch on. Sew buttons on coat of Humpty Dumpty: 3 on front and 2 on back. Make a pom-pom (see page 78) in red for nose. Embroider with a loose loop st. for eyebrows (make a loop and secure with a small stitch).
Note: Do not make loops so large that they will catch.

HAT

Using 3¼ mm (no. 10) needles and red, cast on 91 sts.
Work in k1, p1, rib for 8 cm / 3 in, increasing 1 st on last row. *92 sts.*
Change to 4 mm (no. 8) needles and work in brick st. (see page 7) until work measures 17 cm (6½) in, ending with a WS row and decreasing 1 st. on last row. *91 sts.*

Shape crown
Cont. in st.st.
1st row: * k8, k2tog., rep. from * to last st., k1.
Work 3 rows.
5th row: * k7, k2tog., rep. from * to last st., k1.
Work 3 rows.
9th row: * k6, k2tog., rep from * to last st., k1.
Work 3 rows.
13th row: * k5, k2tog., rep. from * to last st., k1.
Work 3 rows.
17th row: * k4, k2tog., rep. from * to last st., k1.
Work 3 rows.
21st row: * k3, k2tog., rep. from * to last st., k1.
Work 3 rows.
25th row: * k2, k2tog., rep. from * to last st., k1.
Work 3 rows.
29th row: * k1, k2tog., rep. from * to last st., k1.
Break off enough yarn to run through rem. 19 sts. Draw up and fasten off tightly.

Make up
Sew up seam. Lightly press seams. Turn back rib and make a pom-pom (see page 78) with oddments of colour from the jumper. Attach to top of hat.

SOCKS

Using 3¼ mm (no. 10) needles and red, cast on 31 sts.
Work 4 cm / 1½ in in k1, p1, rib, decreasing 1 st. at end of last row.
Change to 4 mm (no. 8) needles and work as follows:
2 rows garter st. in purple.
2 rows st.st. in red.
2 rows garter st. in yellow.
2 rows st.st. in red.
2 rows garter st. in purple.
Cont. in red for 12 rows in st.st.

Shape heel
Next row: k3, turn,
sl.1, p to end.
k5, turn,

sl.1, p to end.
k 7, turn,
sl.1, p to end.
k5, turn,
sl.1, p to end.
k3, turn,
sl.1, p to end.
k to end.
Work other side in same manner, reading p for k and k for p.
Cont. in st.st. working across all sts. until sock measures 19 cm / 7½ in from start, ending on a purl row.

Shape toe
1st row: k6, k2tog., k1, sl.1, k1, psso, k8, k2tog., k1, sl.1, k1, psso, k6.
2nd row: purl.
3rd row: k5, k2tog., k1, sl.1, k1, psso, k6, k2tog., k1, sl.1, k1, psso, k5.
4th row: purl.
5th row: k4, k2tog., k1, sl.1, k1, psso, k4, k2tog., k1, sl.1, k1, psso, k4.
6th row: purl.
Cast off. Join seams and lightly press. Fold rib in half.

GLOVES

To make a pair of gloves for this outfit, follow the pattern on page 22, using 25 g of red.

Toy Humpty Dumpty

MEASUREMENTS

Width round widest part: approx. 70 cm / 28 in
Height when sitting: 33 cm / 13 in

MATERIALS

Wool
The numbers in brackets after the colours refer to Rowan Yarns DK lightweight. Any other double knitting wool can be used provided the tension is the same.

cream (84)	75 g
yellow (13)	50 g
red (42)	25 g
purple (126)	50 g
yarn for embroidering features	

Needles and notions
1 pair 3¼ mm (no. 10) needles; crochet hook; 1 metre / yard ribbon; 3 buttons; kapoc stuffing

TENSION

6 sts. × 8 rows st.st. on 3¼ mm (no. 10) needles makes a 2.5 cm / 1 in square

PATTERN

(See also photograph on page 11.)

Top half
Using 3¼ mm (no. 10) needles and cream, cast on 41 sts. and work 30 rows in st.st., starting with a knit row.
Cont. in st.st., decreasing 1 st. at each end of next and every alt. row until 3 sts. remain.

Next row: purl.
Next row: sl.1, k2tog., psso, fasten off.
Make 3 more pieces the same.

Lower half

With purple yarn, cast on 41 sts. and work 30 rows in garter st.
Change to yellow and cont. in st.st., decreasing 1 st. at each
end of next and every alt. row until 3 sts. remain.
Work 1 row straight.
Next row: sl.1, k2tog., psso, fasten off.
Make 3 more pieces the same.

Arms

With purple yarn, cast on 21 sts. and work 30 rows in garter st.
Change to cream and cont. in st.st. for 10 rows.
Shape as follows:
1st row: [k1, k2tog. tbl, k5, k2tog.] twice, k1.
2nd row: purl.
3rd row: [k1, k2tog. tbl, k3, k2tog.] twice, k1.
4th row: purl.
5th row: [k1, k2tog. tbl, k1, k2tog.] twice, k1.
Cast off.
Make another piece the same.

Legs

With yellow yarn, cast on 21 sts. and work 38 rows in st.st.
Change to red and cont. 6 rows in st.st., starting with a knit
row.
Shape as follows:
1st row: k10, m1(k), k1, m1(k), k10.
2nd row: p11, m1(p), p1, m1(p), p11.
3rd row: k12, m1(k), k1, m1(k), k12.
4th row: p13, m1(p), p1, m1(p), p13.
Cont. in this manner on every row until the row p19, m1(p), p1,
m1(p), p19, has been worked. *41 sts.*
Next row: k1, k2tog. tbl, knit to last 3 sts., k2tog.,k1.
Next row: purl.
Rep. the last 2 rows once more. *37 sts.*
Next row: [k1, k2tog. tbl, k13, k2tog.] twice, k1.
Next row: p14, p2tog. tbl, p1, p2tog., p14.
Next row: [k1, k2tog. tbl, k10, k2tog.] twice, k1.
Cast off.
Make another piece the same.

Make up

With right sides together, join the 4 sections for top half. Join
4 sections of lower half in same way. Lightly press seams.

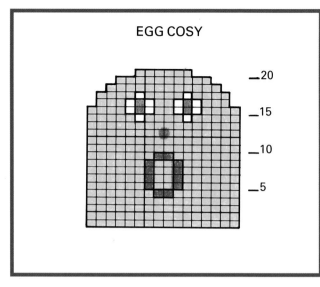

Join top and lower halves together, leaving an opening for the
stuffing. Turn right way out. Stuff firmly, keeping egg shape at
top. Sew up opening. With right sides together, join side
seams on arms and back seams on legs. Lightly press seams.
Leave tops open for stuffing. Turn right way out, stuff and sew
up. Sew legs and arms to body. Make a small red pom-pom
(see page 78) for nose. Embroider features, using a loop st. for
eyebrows.
Tie ribbon round waist and make into a bow. Stitch in place.
Sew buttons on front. Make shoe laces by making 2 crochet
chains 25 cm (10 in) long, using purple. Tie bows in laces and
stitch in place.

Pocket

Using 3¼ mm (no. 10) needles and purple, cast on 16 sts. and
work 12 rows in garter st.
Work 4 rows in k1, p1, rib.
Cast off.
Stitch onto Humpty Dumpty and insert egg cosy.

Egg cosy

Using 3¼ mm (no. 10) needles, follow the chart above for
number of sts., number of rows and colour. Work in st.st. and
knit 2 pieces. With right sides together, sew the two pieces
together. Lightly press. Turn right way out. Embroider face as
shown on chart.

*The toys gathered together for a group picture. Patterns
are on the following pages: musical cushion p. 38;
Humpty Dumpty p. 9; blackbird mobile p. 40; toy mice
p. 74; five squeaky pigs p. 54; Wee Willie Winkie p. 67;
bag and roses p. 47; hot water bottle cover p. 69; hand
puppet p. 23; ball p. 17 and toy lamb p. 62.*

Ladybird, ladybird,
  Fly away home,
Your house is on fire
  And your children all gone;
All except one
  And that's little Ann
And she has crept under
  The warming pan.

Ladybird, Ladybird

A bright red playsuit and hat with black ladybird spots for boy or girl. The matching ball has a soft stuffing to make it a safe toy for younger children and there are bells attached to it to warn all real ladybirds to fly away home.

MEASUREMENTS

Playsuit
Chest: 46 (51, 56) cm / 18 (20, 22) in
Shoulder to crutch: 33 (36, 38) cm / 13 (14, 15) in
Inside leg length (excluding turn-up): 22 (23, 24) cm / 8½ (9, 9½) in

Hat (one size)
Width round head: 37 cm / 14½ in

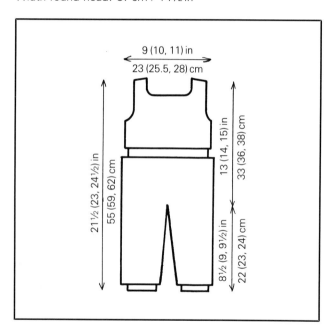

9 (10, 11) in
23 (25.5, 28) cm

13 (14, 15) in
33 (36, 38) cm

21½ (23, 24½) in
55 (59, 62) cm

8½ (9, 9½) in
22 (23, 24) cm

MATERIALS

Wool
The numbers in brackets after the colours refer to Rowan Yarns handknit DK cotton. Any other cotton double knitting can be used provided the tension is the same.

	Playsuit	*Hat*
flame (254)	300 g (350 g, 400 g)	50 g
black (252)	50 g (75 g, 100 g)	50 g

Alternative colourways
A sunshine yellow (271) can be used in place of the red as the main shade. Alternatively, the red and black can be reversed, so that black is the MS.

Needles and notions
1 pair 2¾ mm (no. 12) and 1 pair 3¼ mm (no. 10) needles; 1 × 4 mm (no. 8) crochet hook; 4 buttons (for playsuit); 3 decorative buttons (optional)

TENSION

22 sts. × 28 rows st.st. on 3¼ mm (no. 10) needles makes a 10 cm / 4 in square

PATTERN

When following the chart on page 15, use st.st. for the red background and moss st. for the black spots. (The black band is worked in rib as directed in the instructions.)
Moss stitch: * k1, p1, rep. from * to last st., k1.
Rep. this row until desired length is reached.
Note: for a simpler version, the playsuit can be knitted throughout in st.st.

PLAYSUIT

Back and front

Left leg
Using 2¾ mm (no. 12) needles and red, cast on 23 (25, 27) sts.
Work in k1, p1, rib for 8 cm / 3 in, ending with a RS row.
Next row: p2, [m1, p1] 20 (22, 24) times, p1. *43 (47, 51) sts.*
Change to 3¼ mm (no. 10) needles and follow the chart on page 15 starting at line 1. Cont. until work measures 25 (27, 28) cm / 10 (10½, 11) in, ending with a RS row.
Leave sts. on a thread.

14

PLAYSUIT FRONT & BACK

Black spots in moss st.

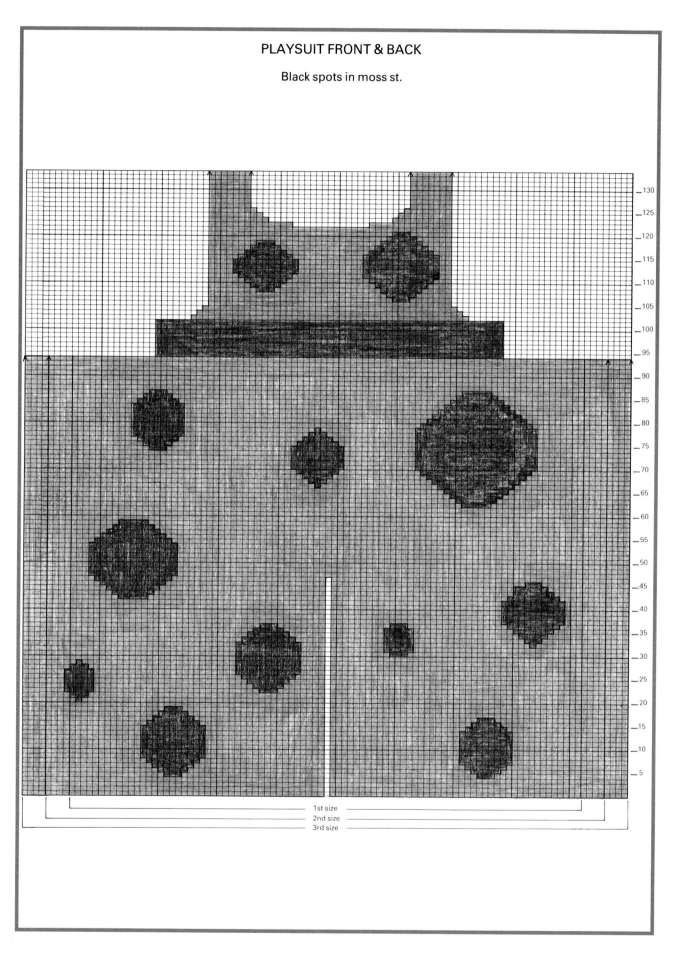

Right leg

Work to match left leg, following chart for position of spots.
Next row: Cont. to work in pattern as shown on the chart. Purl across 43 (47, 51) sts. left on thread for right leg, cast on 1 st. and purl across 43 (47, 51) sts. left on thread for left leg. *87 (95, 103) sts.*

Cont. in st.st. until crutch measures 17 (18, 19) cm / 6½ (7, 7½) in, ending on a RS row.

Next row: (dec. for bodice): **1st size:** p3, * p2tog., p1, rep. from * to end.

Next row: (dec. for bodice): **2nd size:** p6, * p2tog., p1, rep. from * to last 5 sts., p5.

Next row: (dec. for bodice): **3rd size:** p1, * p2tog., p1, rep. from * to end.

Change to 2¾ mm (no. 12) needles and using black, work 8 rows in k1, p1, rib.

Shape armholes

Cast off 6 (7, 5) sts. at beg. of next 2 rows. Change to 3¼ mm (no. 10) needles and red. Dec. 1 st. at each end of every row to 41 (47, 53) sts.
Cont. without shaping until armhole measures 6 (8, 9) cm / 2½ (3, 3½) in, ending on a WS row.

Shape neck

k14 (k16, k18), turn, work on these sts.
Next row: cast off 4 (5, 6) sts., purl to end.
** Dec. 1 st. at neck edge on every row to 7 (8, 9) sts. Cont. without shaping until armhole measures 14 (15, 17) cm / 5½ (6, 6½) in, ending with a WS row.
Leave these sts. on a thread. **
With RS facing, working on rem. 27 (31, 35) sts., slip 13 (15, 17) sts. onto a thread, knit to end.
Next row: purl.
Next row: cast off 5 (6, 7) sts., knit to end.
Work rem. 9 (10, 11) sts. from ** to **.

Borders

Sew up side seams.

Right armhole border

With RS facing, using 2¾ mm (no. 12) needles and red, pick up and knit 81 (85, 89) sts. evenly around armhole edge. Work in moss st. for 2 cm / ½ in.
Cast off in moss st.

Left armhole border

Work to match right armhole border.

Front and back neck border

With RS facing, using 2¾ mm (no. 12) needles and red, pick up and knit 15 (16, 17) sts. down left side of front neck, 13 (15, 17) sts. left on a thread at front neck and 15 (16, 17) sts. up right side of front neck. *43 (47, 51) sts.*
Work in moss st. for 2 cm / ½ in.
Cast off in moss st.

Shoulder borders (all 4 the same)

Using 2¾ mm (no. 12) needles and red, pick up and knit 3 sts. evenly over moss st. border edge, work across 7 (8, 9) sts. left on thread as follows: k 7 (k4, k9), [m1] 0 (1, 0) times, k0 (k4, k0) and pick up and knit 3 sts. evenly over other moss st. border edge. *13 (15, 15) sts.*
Work in moss st. for 2 cm / ½ in.
Cast off in moss st.

Make up

Sew up side and inside leg seams. Press. Using a 4 mm (no. 8) crochet hook, work 2 chain loops on each shoulder on back only (large enough to fit over buttons). Sew on buttons in corresponding positions on front. Fold lower edges of rib onto RS to form turn-ups. Sew on 2 ladybird buttons as decoration.

HAT

Using 4 mm (no. 10) needles and red, follow the chart below in st.st. for red background and in moss st. for the spots as before.
Work from the chart until row 40 (shape crown) has been worked.

Shape crown

Cont. in st.st.

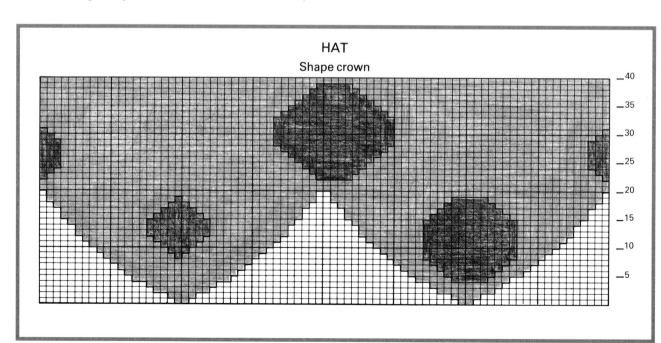

HAT
Shape crown

1st row: * k8, k2tog., rep. from * to last st., k1.
Work 3 rows.
5th row: * k7, k2tog., rep. from * to last st., k1.
Work 3 rows.
9th row: * k6, k2tog., rep. from * to last st., k1.
Work 3 rows.
13th row: * k5, k2tog., rep. from * to last st., k1.
Work 3 rows.
17th row: * k4, k2tog., rep. from * to last st., k1.
Work 3 rows.
21st row: * k3, k2tog., rep. from * to last st., k1.
Work 3 rows.
25th row: * k2, k2tog., rep. from * to last st., k1.
Work 3 rows.
29th row: * k1, k2tog., rep. from * to last st., k1.
Break off yarn, leaving enough to run through rem. 17 sts.
Draw up tightly and fasten off securely.

Make up

Pick up 86 sts. along edge in red. Work 1 row in k1, p1 rib. Cast off in k1, p1, rib. Sew up back seam. Press. Make a tassel and attach to hat with a crochet chain 2.5 cm / 1 in long (see page 78). Sew on ladybird button as decoration.

Ladybird Ball

MEASUREMENTS

Circumference: 47 cm / 18½ in

MATERIALS

Wool

The numbers in brackets after the colours refer to Rowan Yarns handknit DK cotton. Any other cotton double knitting can be used provided the tension is the same.

flame (254)   50 g
black (252)   50 g

Needles and notions

1 pair 3¼ mm (no. 10) needles; 2 bells; kapoc stuffing

TENSION

22 sts. × 28 rows st.st. on 3¼ mm (no. 10) needles makes a 10 cm / 4 in square

PATTERN

(See also photograph on page 11.)

Follow the chart below in st.st. to make 5 pieces.
Work spots as follows:
1st row: knit.
2nd row: p1, k1, to size of spot, ending with a p1.
Continue keeping moss st. correct.
Stitch up the seams to form into a ball, making sure that the black bands match and leaving one end open. Stuff and finish stitching up. Attach bells securely at either end.

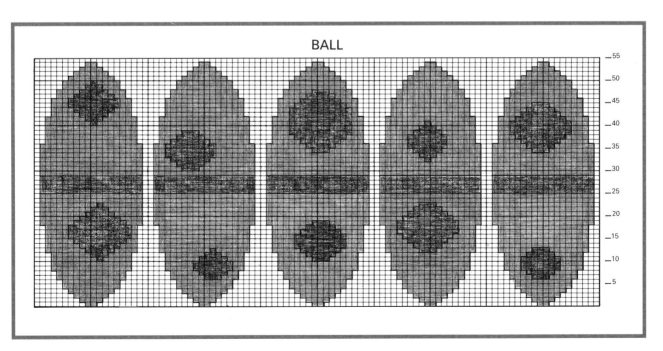

BALL

*L*ittle Jack Horner
Sat in the corner,
Eating a Christmas pie;
He put in his thumb,
And pulled out a plum,
And said, What a good boy am I!

Little Jack Horner

*P*lums made out of pom-poms feature all over this matching outfit of jumper, hat and gloves for boys or girls. More pom-pom plums are to be found inside the pocket which doubles up as the Christmas pie. Little Jack Horner makes another appearance as a hand puppet still with a plum on the end of his thumb.

MEASUREMENTS

Jumper
Chest: 51 (56, 61) cm / 20 (22, 24) in
Length from centre back of neck (without collar): 34 (37, 39) cm / 13½ (14½, 15½) in
Sleeve: 22 (24, 27) cm / 8½ (9½, 10½) in

Hat and gloves
One size: 3–5 years

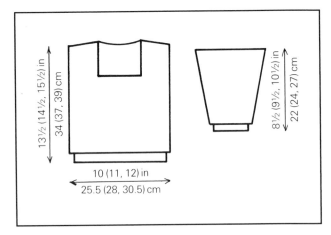

13½ (14½, 15½) in
34 (37, 39) cm

8½ (9½, 10½) in
22 (24, 27) cm

10 (11, 12) in
25.5 (28, 30.5) cm

MATERIALS

Wool
The numbers in brackets after the colours refer to Rowan Yarn shades in lightweight double knitting. Any other double knitting can be used provided the tension is the same.

	Jumper	Hat	Gloves
yellow (13) [MS]	125 g (150 g, 200 g)	50 g	25 g
purple (99)	75 g	oddments	oddments
plum (94)	25 g	oddments	
green (124)	25 g		
red (115)	25 g		
skin (401)	25 g		

Alternative colourway
Use a taupe (58) brown for the main shade in place of the yellow.

Needles and notions
1 pair 3¼ mm (no. 10) and 1 pair 4 mm (no. 8) needles; crochet hook; 1 button

TENSION

24 sts. × 32 rows st.st. on 4 mm (no. 8) needles makes a 10 cm / 4 in square

PATTERN

JUMPER

Back
** Using 3¼ mm (no. 10) needles and MS, cast on 54 (60, 66) sts. Work in k1, p1, rib for 5 (6, 6) cm / 2 (2½, 2½) in.
Next row: (inc.): rib 6 (6, 7) sts., * inc. 1 st., rib 7 (12, 13) sts., rep. from * to last 6 (6, 7) sts., inc. 1 st., rib to end. *61 (65, 71) sts.*
Change to 4 mm (no. 8) needles. Cont. in st.st. until work measures 22 (23, 24) cm / 8½ (9, 9½) in.

Shape armholes
Cast off 2 sts. at beg. of next 2 rows. *57 (61, 67) sts.***

Work straight until armhole measures 13 (14, 15) cm / 5 (5½, 6) in from beg. of shaping, ending on a wrong side row.

Shape shoulders
Cast off 6 (6, 7) sts. at beg. of next 4 rows and 5 (7, 7) sts. at beg. of foll. 2 rows.
Cast off.

Front
Work as for back from ** to ** following the chart below after the rib has been worked and starting at line 1 of the chart.

Divide for neck opening
Knit 17 (19, 21), turn, and leave rem. sts. on spare needle.
Work on 1st set of sts. as follows:
Work straight until front measures the same length as back up to beg. of shoulder shaping, ending at armhole edge.

Shape shoulder
Cast off 6 (6, 7) sts. at beg. of next and foll. alt. rows.
Work 1 row.
Cast off.
With right side facing, join yarn to inner end of sts. on spare needle, cast off next 23 (23, 25) sts., st.st. to end of row. 17 (19, 21) sts.
Complete to match 1st side of neck.
Embroider features on face, eyes in purple and mouth in red.
Make holly berries with red French knots (see page 78).

Sleeves
Using 3¼ mm (no. 10) needles and MS, cast on 34 (36, 40) sts.
Work in k1, p1, rib for 5 (6, 6) cm / 2 (2½, 2½) in.
Next row: (inc.): rib 5 (3, 5) sts. * inc 1 st., rib 6 (5, 5) sts., rep. from * to last 5 (3, 5) sts., inc 1 st., rib to end. 39 (43, 47) sts.
Change to 4 mm (no. 8) needles.
Cont. in st.st. inc. 1 st. at each end of 7th and every foll. 8th row to 45 (49, 53) sts., then at each end of every foll. 8th (10th, 10th) row until there are 51 (55, 61) sts.
Work straight until sleeve measures 22 (24, 27) cm / 8½ (9½, 10½) in from beg.
Cast off.

Pocket
Using 4 mm (no. 8) needles and plum, cast on 25 sts.
Work in st.st. for 26 rows.
Change to 3¼ mm (no. 10) needles and rib 4 rows.
Cast off in rib.

Collar
Using 3¼ mm (no. 10) needles and MS, cast on 143 (151, 163) sts.
Work in rib as follows:
Rib row 1: (right side): k1, * p1, k1, rep. from * to end.
Rib row 2: p1, * k1, p1, rep. from * to end.
Rep. these 2 rows for 11 (11, 13) cm / 4½ (4½, 5) in.
Cast off in rib.

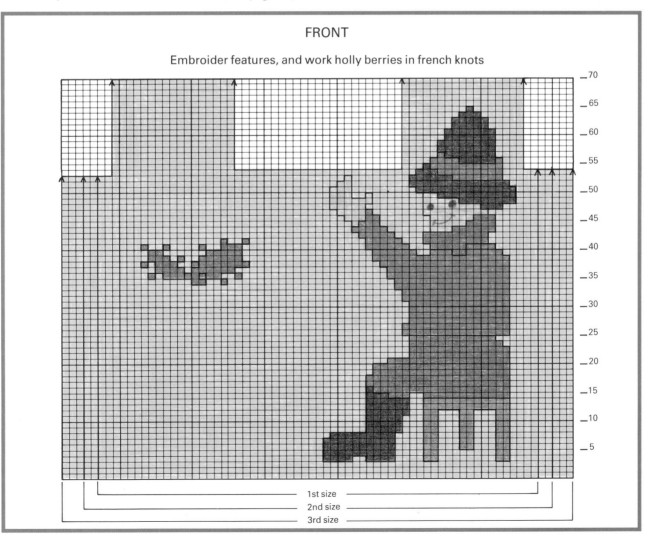

FRONT

Embroider features, and work holly berries in french knots

1st size
2nd size
3rd size

Make up

Join shoulder seams. Sew in sleeves. Join side and sleeve seams. Beginning and ending at inner end of cast off sts. at neck front, sew cast on edge of collar round neck edge. Lapping right side over left for a girl or left over right for a boy, sew row-ends of collar to cast off sts. of front. Stitch pocket into place, gathering it in at the bottom. Lightly press seams. Make 17 pom-poms with purple, using 2.5 cm / 1 in diameter card (see page 78) and attach 13 to jumper. Make different length crochet chains for rem. 4 pom-poms to hang from inside of pocket, attached to the jumper.

Notes: For a simpler version, the plums could be Swiss darned onto the jumper instead of making pom-poms. Leave out the pom-poms in the pocket as a safety precaution if desired.

HAT

Using 3¼ mm (no. 10) needles and MS, cast on 103 sts. Work in k1, p1, rib for 8 cm / 3¼ in.
Change to 4 mm (no. 8) needles and cont. in st.st., starting with a knit row until work measures 20 cm / 8 in, ending with a purl row.
Next row: k3, * k2tog., k3, rep. from * to end. *83 sts.*
Work 3 rows.
Next row: k3, * k2tog., k2, rep. from * to end. *63 sts.*
Work 3 rows.
Next row: k1, * k2tog., rep. from * to end. *32 sts.*
Break off enough yarn to thread through rem. sts. Draw up tightly and fasten off securely.
Make a pom-pom (see page 78), 5 cm / 2 in in diameter with purple and plum mixed.

Ear pieces (make 2)

Using 3¼ mm (no. 10) needles and MS, cast on 17 sts. and work in k1, p1, rib for 4 cm / 1¾ in.
Dec. 1 st. at each end of every row until 5 sts. remain.
One side only: cont. for 10 cm / 4 in.
Cast off in rib.
Make chain buttonhole at long end.

Make up

Join seams, reversing the seam for 8 cm / 3¼ in for turn-back. Fold back ribbing, then fold again to form a double brim. Sew ear pieces to lower edge of brim. Sew on button. Sew on pom-pom.

GLOVES

Right glove

** Using 3¼ mm (no. 10) needles and MS, cast on 31 sts. Work in k1, p1, rib for 8 cm / 3¼ in.
Next row: rib 6 sts., [m1, rib 10 sts.] twice, m1, rib to end. *34 sts.*
Starting with a knit row, work 2 rows in st.st. **
*** Shape thumb gusset as follows:
Next row: k18, m1, k1, m1, knit to end.
Work 3 rows.
Next row: k18, m1, k3, m1, knit to end.
Work 3 rows.
Next row: k18, m1, k5, m1, knit to end.
Cont. increasing 1 st. at each side of thumb gusset as before on every foll. 4th row until there are 42 sts.
Work 1 row. ***
Work thumb as follows:
1st row: k28, turn,
2nd row: p10, cast on 2 sts., turn,
Work 5 rows on these 12 sts. Join in purple and cont. for

another 5 rows.
Shape top as follows:
1st row: * k2tog., rep. from * to end.
2nd row: purl.
Break off enough yarn to thread through rem. sts. Draw up tightly and fasten off securely.
Join seam.
**** With right side facing, rejoin MS and knit up 2 sts. from cast on sts. at base of thumb, knit 14. *34 sts.*
Next row: k21, k2tog., k1, k2tog., knit to end. *32 sts.*
Work 7 rows. ****

Divide for 1st finger

Next row: k22, turn,
Next row: p10, cast on 2 sts., turn,
Work 9 rows on these 12 sts. Join in purple and cont. for another 5 rows.
Shape top as follows:
1st row: * k2tog., rep. from * to end.
2nd row: purl.
Complete as for thumb.

2nd finger

With right side facing, rejoin MS and knit up 2 sts. from cast on sts. at base of 1st finger, knit 4, turn,
Next row: p10, cast on 2 sts., turn,
Work 11 rows on these 12 sts. Join in purple and cont. for another 5 rows.
Shape top as for 1st finger.
Complete as for thumb.

3rd finger

With right side facing, rejoin MS and knit up 2 sts. from cast on sts. at base of 2nd finger, knit 4, turn,
Next row: p10, cast on 2 sts., turn,
Work 9 rows on these 12 sts. Join in purple and cont. for another 5 rows.
Shape top as for 1st finger.
Complete as for thumb.

4th finger

With right side facing, rejoin MS and knit up 2 sts. from cast on sts. at base of 3rd finger, knit to end.
Next row: purl.
Work 5 rows on these 10 sts. Join in purple and cont. for another 5 rows.
Shape top as for 1st finger.
Complete as for thumb, sewing seam to cast on edge, reversing seam for 4 cm / 1½ in on cuff to turn back.

Left glove

Work as right glove from ** to **.
*** Shape thumb gusset as follows:
Next row: k15, m1, k1, m1, knit to end.
Work 3 rows.
Next row: k15, m1, k3, m1, knit to end.
Work 3 rows.
Next row: k15, m1, k5, m1, knit to end.
Cont. inc. 1 st. at each side of thumb gusset as before on every foll. 4th row until there are 42 sts.
Work 1 row. ***
Work thumb as follows:
1st row: k24, turn and cast on 2 sts.
Next row: p12, turn,
Complete as for thumb of right glove.
**** With right side facing, rejoin MS and knit up 2 sts. from cast on sts. at base of thumb, knit 18. *34 sts.*
Next row: k17, k2tog., k1, k2tog., knit to end. *32 sts.*

Work 7 rows as right glove.
Divide for 1st finger as follows:
Next row: k22, cast on 2 sts., turn,
Next row: p12, turn,
Complete as for 1st finger of right glove.

2nd finger
With right side facing, rejoin MS and knit up 2 sts. from cast on sts. at base of 1st finger, knit 4, turn and cast on 2 sts.
Next row: p12, turn,
Complete as for 2nd finger of right glove.

3rd finger
With right side facing, rejoin MS and knit up 2 sts. from cast on sts. at base of 2nd finger, knit 4, turn and cast on 2 sts.
Next row: p12, turn,
Complete as for 3rd finger of right glove.

4th finger
Work as for 4th finger on right glove.

Hand Puppet

MATERIALS

Wool
The numbers in brackets after the colours refer to Rowan Yarn shades in lightweight double knitting. Any other double knitting can be used provided the tension is the same.

yellow (13)	25 g
purple (99)	oddments
plum (94)	oddments
brown (87)	oddments
red (115)	oddments
skin (401)	oddments

Needles and notions
1 pair 3¼ mm (no. 10) needles; crochet hook; 3 buttons; kapoc stuffing

TENSION

28 sts. × 36 rows st.st. on 3¼ mm (no. 10) needles makes a 10 cm / 4 in square

PATTERN

(See also photograph on page 11.)

Glove
Using 3¼ mm (no. 10) needles and yellow, cast on 42 sts.
Work in k1, p1, rib for 5 rows.
Cont. in st.st. for 16 rows, starting with a knit row and ending with a purl row.

Shape thumb gusset
1st row: k22, m1, k1, m1, knit to end.
Work 3 rows in st.st.
5th row: k22, m1, k3, m1, knit to end.
Work 3 rows in st.st.
9th row: k22, m1, k5, m1, knit to end.
Cont. increasing 1 st. at each side of thumb gusset as before on every foll. 4th row until there are 52 sts.
Work 5 rows in st.st.
Work thumb as follows:
1st row: k34, turn,
2nd row: p12, cast on 4 sts., turn,

Work 10 rows in st.st. on these 16 sts.
Change to skin and cont. for 4 rows on these 16 sts.

Shape top
1st row: * k2tog., rep. from * to end.
2nd row: purl.
Break off enough yarn to thread through rem. sts. Draw up tightly and fasten off securely.
Join seam.
With RS facing, rejoin yellow yarn and knit up 4 sts. from cast on sts. at base of thumb, knit 18. *44 sts.*
Work 1 row.
Next row: k21, k2tog., k1, k2tog., knit to end. *42 sts.*
Work 9 rows.
Work 32 sts., turn, leave rem. 10 sts. on spare needle.
Cont. in st.st. for 8 rows.
Change to red and work 2 rows.
Change to skin and work 10 rows.

Shape top
1st row: dec. 2 sts. at each end of row.
2nd row: purl.
Cont. to dec. 4 sts. in this way on every alt. row until 16 sts. rem., ending with a purl row.
Cast off.

4th finger
With RS facing, rejoin yellow yarn, cast on 3 sts. at base of centre of hand and knit up 10 sts. on spare needle. *13 sts.*
Cont. in st.st. for 11 rows on these 13 sts.

Shape top
1st row: k1, * k2tog., rep. from * to end.
2nd row: purl.
Break off enough yarn to thread through rem. sts. Draw up tightly and fasten off securely. With right sides together, join seam and turn right way out.

Pocket
Using plum, cast on 14 sts.
Work in st.st. for 16 rows.
Work in k1, p1, rib for 4 rows.
Cast off.

Hat (make 2 pieces)
Using purple, cast on 25 sts.
Work 2 rows in k1, p1, rib, dec. 1 st. at each end of both rows.
Work 4 rows in st.st., dec. as above. *15 sts.*
Work 2 rows.
Change to red and work 2 rows.
Rejoin purple and work 14 rows in st.st.
Next row: * k2tog., rep. from * to last st., k1.
Next row: purl.
Break off yarn and draw up tightly. Fasten off. With right sides together, stitch 2 pieces together at seams. Turn right way out.

Make up
Stitch pocket into place. Make 2 pom-poms (see page 78). Put one on a crochet chain and hang from pocket and stitch the other to end of puppet's thumb. Sew 3 buttons down front. Embroider face with red mouth and plum eyes. Make hair with brown yarn doubled, stitching large loops round head area (make a large loop and secure with a small st.).
Lightly stuff hat and stitch onto head.

Hey diddle, diddle,
The cat and the fiddle,
The cow jumped over the moon;
The little dog laughed
To see such sport,
And the dish ran away with the spoon.

Hey Diddle Diddle

All the crazy characters of this nursery rhyme are knitted into these dungarees and cardigan designed for boys or girls. Mittens with cat faces complete the outfit. The laughing dog, jumping cow, running dish and spoon and the fiddling cat are also knitted from the same charts to make a mobile for the nursery.

MEASUREMENTS

Dungarees
Length from bib to bottom: 48 (51, 54) cm / 19 (20, 21½) in
Inside leg: 23 (24, 26) cm / 9 (9½, 10) in

Cardigan
Chest: 46 (51, 56) cm / 18 (20, 22) in
Length from centre back of neck: 27 (29, 32) cm / 10½ (11½, 12½) in
Sleeve: 14 (17, 19) cm / 5½ (6½, 7½) in

Mittens
Size: 1–3 years (4–5 years)

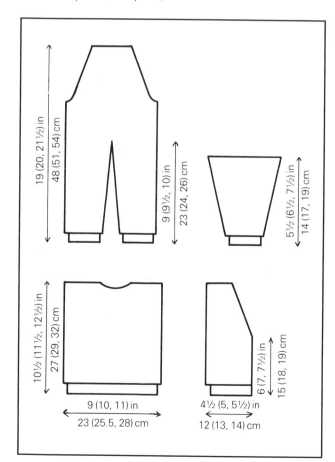

MATERIALS

Wool
The numbers in brackets after the colours refer to Rowan Yarn shades in lightweight double knitting. Any other double knitting can be used provided the tension is the same.

	Dungarees	Cardigan	Mittens
pale green (75)	125 g (150 g, 200 g)	100 g (125 g, 175 g)	oddments
dark green (124)	25 g	25 g	25 g
cream (2)	25 g (or oddments)	oddments	oddments
grey (61)	25 g (or oddments)	oddments	
pink (19)	oddments	25 g	
yellow (12)	oddments	25 g	
brown (104)	oddments	25 g	
black (62)	oddments	25 g	oddments
red (115)	25 g (or oddments)	oddments	oddments

Alternative colourway
Use a pale royal blue (55) in place of the pale green and royal blue (57) in place of the dark green as shown on contents pages.

Needles and notions
1 pair 3¼ mm (no. 10) and 1 pair 4 mm (no. 8) needles; 3 bells (optional); 6 buttons

TENSION

24 sts. × 32 rows st.st. on 4 mm (no. 8) needles makes a 10 cm / 4 in square

PATTERN

DUNGAREES

Follow the charts for back and front on pages 28 and 29, starting at line 1, after rib has been worked.

Legs (make 4)

Using 3¼ mm (no. 10) needles and dark green, cast on 19 (21, 23) sts.

Work in k1, p1, rib for 5 rows.

Next row: (inc.): rib 1 (2, 3) sts., * m1, rib 2, m1, rib 1, rep. from * to last 0 (1, 2) sts., rib 0 (1, 2) sts. *31 (33, 35) sts.*

Change to 4 mm (no. 8) needles and pale green. Starting with a knit row, work in st.st. until leg measures 23 (24, 26) cm / 9 (9½, 10) in, ending with a purl row.

Leave sts. on a stitch holder.

Back and front

Using 4 mm (no. 8) needles, knit across 31 (33, 35) sts. of one leg, turn, cast on 7 (9, 9) sts., turn, knit across 31 (33, 35) sts. of second leg. *69 (75, 79) sts.*

Next row: purl.

Following the charts on page 28 and 29, cont. in st.st., dec. 1 st. at each end of 2nd (4th, 6th) and every foll. 8th (6th, 6th) row until 57 (59, 63) sts. remain.

Work straight until piece measures 18 (19, 20) / 7 (7½, 8) in, ending with a purl row.

Next row: k2, [p1, k1] twice, k1, slip these 7 sts. onto a safety pin, knit to last 7 sts., turn and leave rem. 7 sts., on a safety pin. *43 (45, 49) sts.*

Next row: purl.

Shape bib

Cont. in st.st., dec. 1 st. at each end of next and every foll. alt. row until 29 (31, 33) sts. remain.

Work 1 row.

Change to 3¼ mm (no. 10) needles and dark green.

Work in k1, p1, rib for 2.5 cm / 1 in.

Cast off in rib.

Left front border

* With wrong side facing, using 3¼ mm (no. 10) needles and dark green, rejoin yarn to inside edge of 7 sts. on safety pin and work in rib as follows:

1st row: k1, [p1, k1] 3 times.

2nd row: k2, [p1, k1] twice, k1.

Rep. these 2 rows until border, when slightly stretched, fits up side of bib to top of ribbing, ending with a 1st row. Sew in position as you go along. *

Cast off in rib.

Right front border

With right side facing, using 3¼ mm (no. 10) needles and dark green, rejoin yarn to inside edge of 7 sts. on safety pin and starting with a 2nd row, work as for left front border.

Right back border and strap

Work as given for left front border from * to *. Cont. in rib and work a further 13 (14, 15) cm / 5 (5½, 6) in, ending with a 2nd row.

Next row: (buttonhole): rib 3 sts., yrn, p2tog., rib 2 sts.

Work 4 rows in rib.

Cast off in rib.

Left back border and strap

With right side facing, using 3¼ mm (no. 10) needles and dark green, rejoin yarn to inside edge of 7 sts. on safety pin, starting with a 2nd row.

Work as for right back border.

Make up

Join leg and side seams. Press seams. Sew on buttons to top of front bib. Work Swiss darning and embroidery (see page 78) as shown on the charts. Loop strands of yarn to make whiskers, attaching firmly to cat. Press. If liked, sew bells on boots of cat.

CARDIGAN

Follow charts for back, fronts and sleeve on pages 30 to 31.

Back

Using 3¼ mm (no. 10) needles and dark green, cast on 61 (67, 73) sts.

Work in k1, p1, rib for 4 cm / 1½ in.

Change to 4 mm (no. 8) needles and pale green. Cont. in st.st. until work measures 27 (29, 32) cm / 10½ (11½, 12½) in, ending on wrong side.

Shape shoulders

Cast off 6 (7, 8) sts. at beg. of next 4 rows.

Cast off 7 (8, 9) sts. at beg. of next 2 rows.

Cast off rem. 23 sts.

Work embroidery and Swiss darning.

Left front

* Using 3¼ mm (no. 10) needles and dark green, cast on 29 (31, 35) sts.

Work in k1, p1, rib for 4 cm / 1½ in.

Change to 4 mm (no. 8) needles and pale green.

Following the chart on page 30, cont. in st.st. until work measures 15 (18, 19) cm / 6 (7, 7½) in, ending on wrong side. *

Shape front

Next row: sl.1, knit to last 2 sts., k2tog.

Next row: purl.

Work 18 (23, 26) rows, dec. once at front edge on 1st (2nd, 2nd) and every foll. 2nd (3rd, 3rd) row. *19 (22, 25) sts.*

Cont. without shaping until work measures same as back, ending on wrong side.

Shape shoulder

Next row: cast off 6 (7, 8) sts., knit to end.

Next row: purl.

Next row: cast off 6 (7, 8) sts., knit to end.

Next row: purl.

Cast off rem. 7 (8, 9) sts.

Work Swiss darning.

Right front

Same as left front from * to *.

Shape front

Next row: k2tog., knit to end.

Next row: purl.

Work 18 (23, 26) rows, dec. once on front edge on 1st (2nd, 2nd) and every foll. 2nd (3rd, 3rd) row. *19 (22, 25) sts.*

Cont. without shaping until work measures same as back ending on the right side.

Shape shoulder

Next row: cast off 6 (7, 8) sts., purl to end.

Next row: knit.

Next row: cast off 6 (7, 8) sts., purl to end.

Next row: knit.

Cast off rem. 7 (8, 9) sts.

Work Swiss darning.

Sleeves

Using 3¼ mm (no. 10) needles and dark green, cast on 33 (35, 37) sts.

DUNGAREES FRONT
Swiss darn nose, ribbon, black on head, musical notes, and fiddle

Embroider rest of features on face   Dotted line for mobile

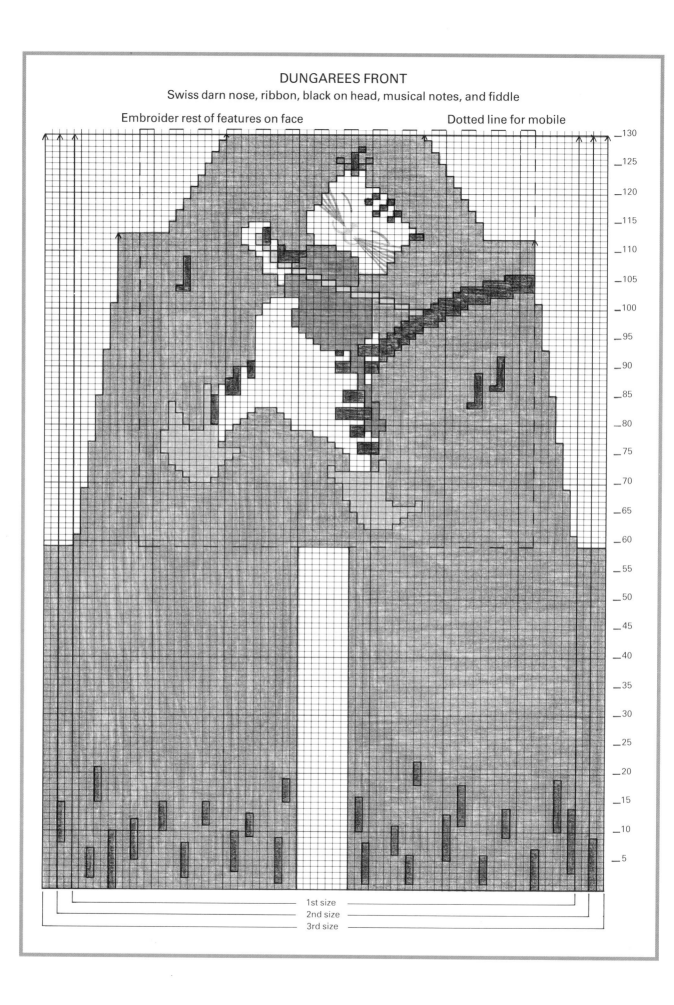

1st size
2nd size
3rd size

DUNGAREES BACK
Swiss darn bow on end of tail or tie with ribbon

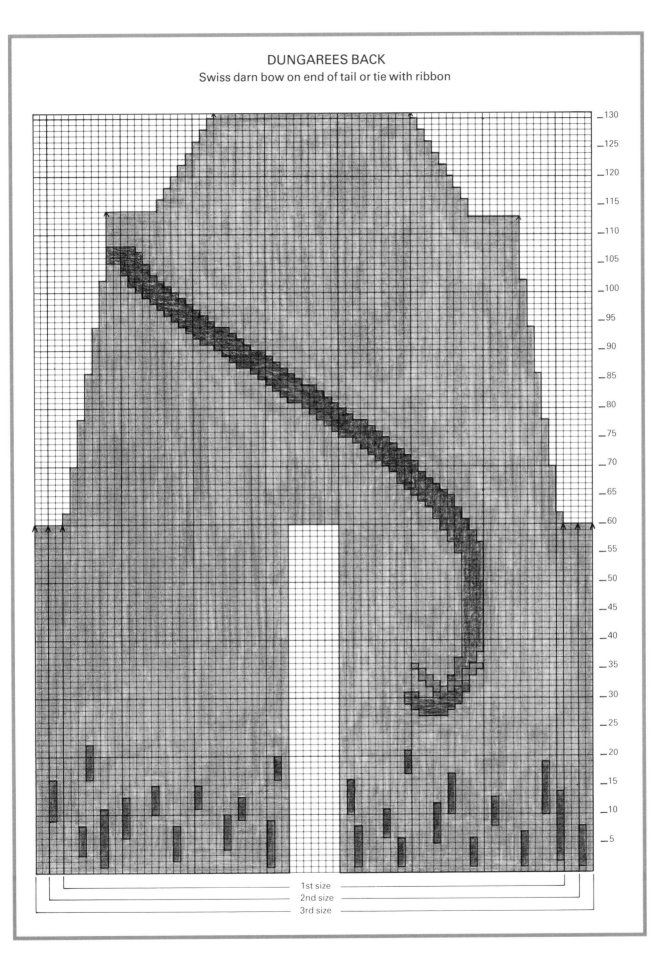

1st size
2nd size
3rd size

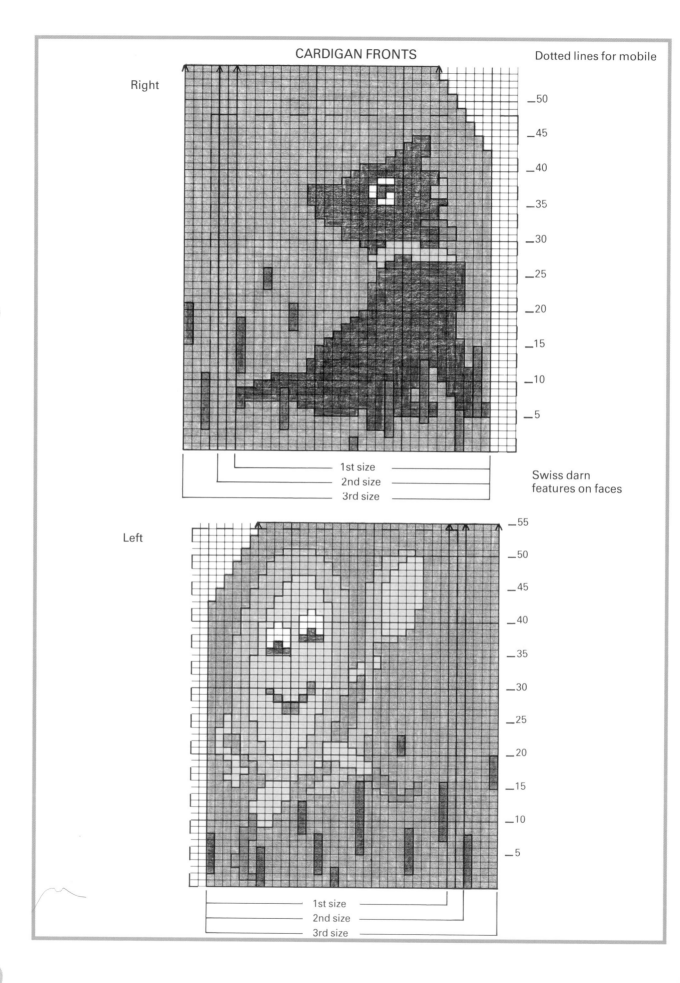

CARDIGAN FRONTS

Right

Dotted lines for mobile

—50
—45
—40
—35
—30
—25
—20
—15
—10
—5

1st size
2nd size
3rd size

Swiss darn
features on faces

Left

—55
—50
—45
—40
—35
—30
—25
—20
—15
—10
—5

1st size
2nd size
3rd size

CARDIGAN SLEEVE

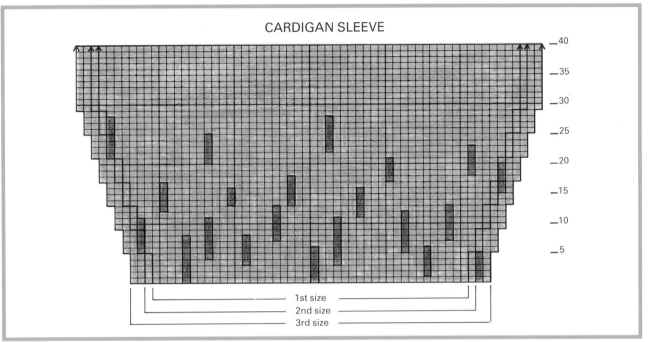

1st size
2nd size
3rd size

CARDIGAN BACK

Swiss darn eyes, bow, hooves and white of tail
Embroider nostrils and mouth on cow's face

Make tassel for end of tail
Dotted line for mobile

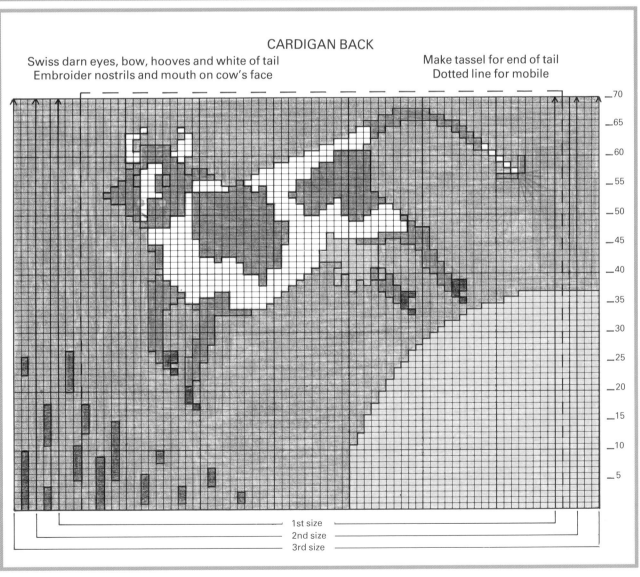

1st size
2nd size
3rd size

Work in k1, p1, rib for 4 cm / 1½ in.
Size 46 (51) cm / 20 (22) in only: inc. 9 sts. evenly along next row. *42 (44) sts.*
Sizes 56 cm / 24 in only: inc. 11 sts. evenly along next row. *48 sts.*
Change to 4 mm (no. 8) needles and pale green. Following chart on page 31, cont. in st.st., inc. once at each end of 5th and every foll. 4th (4th, 4th) row to 48 (54, 60) sts.
Cont. without shaping until work measures 14 (17, 19) cm / 5½ (6½, 7½) in, ending on wrong side. Cast off.

Make up
Sew up shoulder and sleeve seams. Sew up side seams leaving 10 (11, 13) cm / 4 (4½, 5) in free to form armholes. Sew in sleeves. Press seams. Make tassel (see page 78) in grey, brown and cream 4 cm / 1½ in long. Stitch onto end of cow's tail on back. Work embroidery and Swiss darning. If liked, sew bell at cow's neck on back.
Note: The tassel can be omitted for a young child, as a safety precaution.

Buttonhole border (Girls)
Using 3¼ mm (no. 10) needles and dark green, cast on 9 sts.
1st row: sl.1, [k1, p1] 3 times, k2.
2nd row: sl.1, [p1, k1] 4 times.
**** 3rd row:** sl.1, k1, p1, k1, cast off 2 sts., k2.
4th row: sl.1, p1, k1, cast on 2 sts., [p1, k1] twice.
Rep. 1st and 2nd rows 5 (7, 8) times. **
Rep. from ** to ** twice.
Work 3rd and 4th rows once, then 1st and 2nd rows until border is long enough to go up front and halfway across back of neck ending with a 2nd row. Cast off in rib.

Button border (Girls)
Work exactly as buttonhole border omitting buttonholes.

Buttonhole border (Boys)
Using 3¼ mm (no. 10) needles and dark green, cast on 9 sts.
1st row: sl.1, [k1, p1] 3 times, k2.
2nd row: sl.1, [p1, k1] 4 times.
**** 3rd row:** sl.1, k1, p1, cast off 2 sts., p1, k2.
4th row: sl.1, p1, k1, p1, cast on 2 sts., k1, p1, k1.
Rep. 1st and 2nd rows 5 (7, 8) times. ***
Rep. from *** to *** twice, 3rd and 4th rows once, then 1st and 2nd rows until border is long enough to go up front and halfway across back of neck, ending with a 2nd row. Cast off in rib.

Button border (Boys)
Work exactly as buttonhole border omitting buttonholes.

Make up
Sew ends of borders together and placing seam to centre back of neck, sew front borders in position. Press. Sew on buttons to correspond to buttonholes.

MITTENS

Right hand
Using 3¼ mm (no. 10) needles and dark green, cast on 31 (35) sts.
1st row: (right side): k1, * p1, k1, rep. from * to end.
2nd row: p1, * k1, p1, rep. from * to end.
Rep. the last 2 rows until rib measures 4 (5) cm / 1½ (2) in, ending with a wrong side row and increasing 3 sts. evenly across last row. *34 (38) sts.*
Change to 4 mm (no. 8) needles.
Work 4 rows in st.st., starting with a knit row. *

Shape thumb gusset
1st row: k17 (19), m1, k3, m1, knit to end.
Work 3 rows st.st.
5th row: k17 (19), m1, k5, m1, knit to end.
6th row: purl.
7th row: k17 (19), m1, k7, m1, knit to end.
Cont. to inc. 2 sts. in this way on every alt. row until the row: k17 (19), m1, k11, m1, knit to end, has been worked. *44 (48) sts.*
Next row: purl.

Divide for thumb
1st row: k30 (32), turn,
**** 2nd row:** p13, turn,
Work straight on these 13 sts. until thumb measures 2 (3) cm / ¾ (1¼) in, ending with a purl row.
Next row: k1, * k2tog., rep. from * to end.
Break off enough yarn to thread through rem. 7 sts. Draw up tightly and fasten off securely.
With right side of work facing, rejoin yarn at base of thumb and knit to end. *31 (35) sts.*
Work straight until mitten measures 5 (6) cm / 2 (2½) in from division for thumb, ending with a purl row.
Shape top as follows:
1st row: k1, [sl.1(k), k1, psso, k10 (12), k2tog., k1] twice. *27 (31) sts.*
2nd row: purl.
3rd row: k1, [sl.1(k), k1, psso, k8 (10), k2tog., k1] twice. *23 (27) sts.*
Cont. to dec. 4 sts. in this way on every alt. row until 19 sts. remain, ending with a purl row. Cast off. ***

Ears (make 8: 4 in dark green and 4 in pale green)
Using 4 mm (no. 8) needles, cast on 9 sts. and work 4 rows in st.st., starting with a knit row.
Dec. 1 st. at each end of next and foll. 2 alt. rows. *3 sts.*
Next row: purl.
Next row: sl.1(k), k2tog., psso. Fasten off.

Left hand
As for right hand to *.
Shape thumb gusset as follows:
1st row: k14 (16), m1, k3, m1, knit to end.
Work 3 rows in st.st.
5th row: k14 (16), m1, k5, m1, knit to end.
6th row: purl.
7th row: k14 (16), m1, k7, m1, knit to end.
Cont. to inc. 2 sts. in this way on every alt. row until the row: k14 (16), m1, k11, m1, knit to end, has been worked. *44 (48) sts.*
Next row: purl.
Divide for thumbs as follows:
1st row: k27 (29), turn,
Work as given for right hand from ** to ***.

Make up
Join thumbs, top and side seams. Press. With right sides together, sew a dark green to a light green ear, turn right way out, press and sew in place. Rep. for other ears. With oddments of yarn embroider cat features.

HAT

Using an extra 50 g of dark green, follow patt. for 'Little Jack Horner' on page 22 without the ear pieces. Make a green crochet chain 7.3 cm / 3 in long (see page 78) to hang the pom-pom from.

Hey Diddle Diddle Mobile

MEASUREMENTS

Cat and fiddle: 22.5 cm / 9 in square
Cow/moon: 22.5 × 28 cm / 9 × 11 in
Dog: 15 × 14 cm / 6 × 5½ in
Dish/spoon: 18 × 14 cm / 7 × 5½ in

MATERIALS

Wool

The numbers in brackets after the colours refer to Rowan Yarn shades in lightweight double knitting. Any other double knitting can be used provided the tension is the same.

pale green (75)   200 g

rest of colours, use leftovers from cardigan and dungarees patterns or 25 g of each

Needles and notions

1 pair 4 mm (no. 8) needles; 4 bells; ribbon for bow, 3 mm / ⅛ in wide; 1.5 metres / 5 feet of 3 mm / ⅛ in wooden dowling; red paint; glue

TENSION

24 sts. × 32 rows st.st. on 4 mm (no. 8) needles makes a 10 cm / 4 in square

PATTERN

Follow the charts for characters on cardigan and dungaree patterns, working only the areas within the dotted lines. Knit each character (cat/fiddle; cow/moon; laughing dog; dish/spoon) twice in st.st., except for the cat/fiddle where there is a separate chart below for the back.

With right sides tog. stitch side and top seams. Turn right way out and stitch along bottom seam. Sew on bells, cow's tail, cat's bow and cat's whiskers as given in pattern. Press each piece flat.

Make up

Cut 4 pieces of 3 mm dowling slightly longer than the 4 knitted pieces. Cut another piece 40 cm / 16 in long and a final piece 25 cm / 10 in long. Paint all the pieces red. When dry, attach 15 cm / 6 in lengths of pale green yarn to each top corner of the 4 knitted pieces. Tie these to the ends of the 4 pieces of dowling cut to fit. This will hold the pieces flat.

Take the 25 cm / 10 in piece of wood and suspend the little dog 13 cm / 5 in below one end and the cat and fiddle 5 cm / 2 in below the other. Hang this piece of wood by its balancing point 35 cm / 14 in below the middle of the 40 cm / 16 in piece. Suspend the plate and spoon 5 cm / 2 in below one end of this and the cow 10 cm / 4 in below the other end.

Hang the mobile from the ceiling and adjust all the knots, so that the balance is perfect. Trim off the ends of wool and dab a small blob of glue to each knot to fix it.

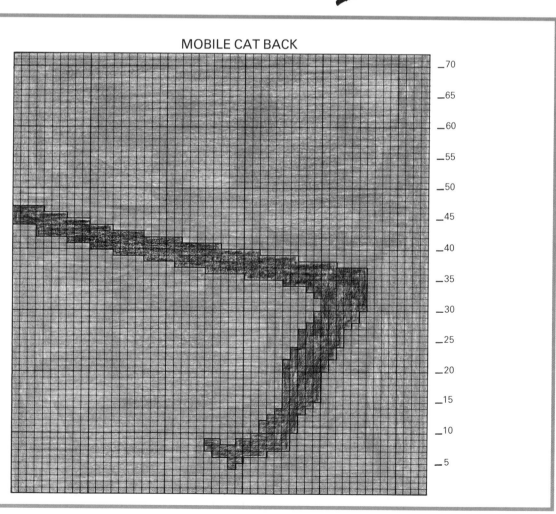

MOBILE CAT BACK

—70
—65
—60
—55
—50
—45
—40
—35
—30
—25
—20
—15
—10
—5

Sing a song of sixpence,
A pocket full of rye;
Four and twenty blackbirds,
Baked in a pie.

When the pie was opened,
The birds began to sing;
Wasn't that a dainty dish,
To set before the king.

Sing a Song of Sixpence

A jumper for boy or girl showing one of the four and twenty blackbirds singing from the pie. Both the jumper and the beret are decorated with more of the blackbirds and are matched with a musical cushion on the same theme. Five of the escaped blackbirds have found their way to a nursery mobile.

MEASUREMENTS

Jumper
Chest: 51 (56, 61) cm / 20 (22, 24) in
Length from centre back of neck: 28 (30, 33) / 11 (12, 13) in
Sleeve: 18.5 (22.5, 29) cm / 7½ (10, 11½) in

Beret
Size: 2–3 years (4–5 years)

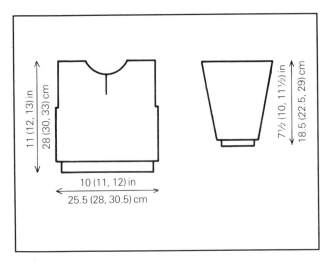

MATERIALS

Wool
The numbers in brackets after the colours refer to Rowan Yarn shades in Botany 4 ply. Any other 4 ply wool can be used provided the tension is the same.

	Jumper	*Beret*
turquoise (125)	75 g (125 g, 175 g)	25 g (50 g)
black (62)	25 g	oddments
orange (17)	50 g (75 g, 100 g)	oddments

Alternative colourway
Use bright pink (621) as shown on contents pages or emerald green (125) in place of the turquoise.

Needles and notions
1 pair 2¾ mm (no. 12) and 1 pair mm 3¼ (no. 10) needles; crochet hook; kapoc stuffing; 2 (3, 3) buttons for jumper; 2 buttons for beret

TENSION

28 sts. × 36 rows st.st. on 3¼ mm (no. 10) needles makes a 10 cm / 4 in square

PATTERN

Note: For a simpler version, the birds attached to the jumper could be omitted and a black pom-pom (see page 78) could be made for the top of the beret.

JUMPER

Back
Using 2¾ mm (no. 12) needles and orange, cast on 71 (75, 83) sts. Work in k1, p1, rib for 5 cm / 2 in, ending on a RS row. Change to 3¼ mm (no. 10) needles and cont. in st.st. following the chart on page 37 for the design, starting at line 1, until work measures 28 (30, 33) cm / 11 (12, 13) in. Cast off. Work Swiss darning (see page 78).

Front
Work exactly as back following the same chart, until work measures 11 (13, 14) cm / 4½ (5, 5½) in less than back, ending on a RS row.

Divide for front opening

Knit 32 (34, 38) sts., cast off 7 sts., knit to end.
Working on first 32 (34, 38) sts., proceed as follows:
** Cont. without shaping until work measures 5 cm / 2 in less than back, ending at neck edge.

Shape neck

Cast off 3 (3, 4) sts., knit to end. **
*** Dec. 1 st. at neck edge in next and every alt. row until 23 (25, 28) sts. remain.
Cont. without shaping until work measures same as back.
Cast off. ***
With right side facing, work rem. 32 (34, 38) sts. from ** to **.
Next row: knit to end.
Work rem. 29 (31, 34) sts. from *** to ***.
Swiss darn musical notes and blackbird's eye.

Sleeves

Using 2¾ mm (no. 12) needles and turquoise, cast on 37 (39, 41) sts.
Work in k1, p1, rib for 12 rows in the sequence: 3 rows turquoise, 2 rows orange, 3 rows turquoise, 2 rows orange, 2 rows turquoise.
Next row: cont. in turquoise, rib 1 (5, 1) sts., m1, [rib 2 sts., m1, rib 2 (1, 1) sts., m1] 8 (9, 12) times, rib 2 sts., m1, rib to end. *55 (59, 67) sts.*
Change to 3¼ mm (no. 10) needles and cont. in st.st. until work measures 18 (19, 20) cm / 7 (7½, 8) in.
Cast off.

Borders
Buttonhole border
With right side facing, using 2¾ mm (no. 12) needles and

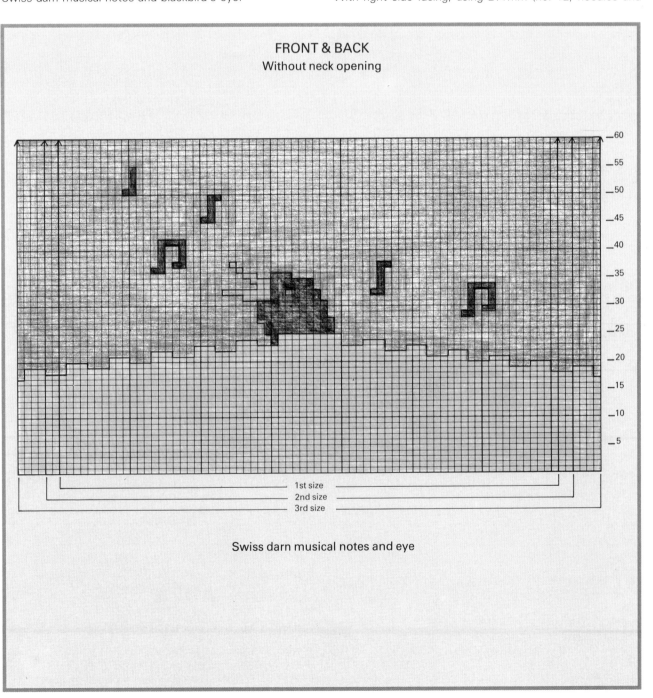

Swiss darn musical notes and eye

FRONT & BACK
Without neck opening

1st size
2nd size
3rd size

55
50
45
40
35
30
25
20
15
10
5

turquoise, pick up and knit 23 (29, 33) sts. along right front edge for girls or left front edge for boys.
Working buttonholes in 5th and 6th rows (see below), work in rib for 3 rows turquoise, 2 rows orange, 3 rows turquoise, 2 rows orange, 2 rows turquoise.
5th row: rib 3 sts., cast off 2 sts., [rib 11 (7, 9) sts., cast off 2 sts] 1 (2, 2) times, rib to end.
6th row: rib 4 sts., cast on 2 sts., [rib 12 (8, 10) sts., cast on 2 sts.] 1 (2, 2) times, rib to end.
Cast off in rib.

Button border

Work as buttonhole border leaving out buttonholes on 5th and 6th rows.

Make up and collar

Sew up shoulder seams. With right side facing, using 2¾ mm (no. 12) needles and turquoise, pick up and knit 23 (23, 24) sts. up right side of neck, 49 (49, 53) sts. evenly across cast off sts. at back of neck and 23 (23, 24) sts. down left side of neck. 95 (95, 101) sts.
Rib for 20 rows in turquoise, then 10 more rows in the sequence: 2 rows orange, 3 rows turquoise, 2 rows orange, 3 rows turquoise.
Cast off in rib.
Place centre of sleeve top at shoulder seam. Sew in position along back and front edges. Sew up rem. seams. Sew borders in position. Lightly press seams on wrong side. Sew on buttons to correspond to buttonholes.

Blackbirds

Make 6 birds. Either sew them straight onto the jumper (which is more secure for a younger child) or make a crochet chain (see page 78) 2.5 cm / 1 in long and hang birds from this chain, so that they appear to fly.
Using 3¼ mm (no. 10) needles and black, knit up 1 wing of large blackbird patt. (see page 40). Sew part of seam and stuff, finish seam. Embroider eye and beak as for large bird patt., using 6 twists for french knots of beak.

BERET

Using 2¾ mm (no. 12) needles and turquoise, cast on 99 (103) sts.
Work in k1, p1, rib for 12 rows in the sequence: 3 rows turquoise, 2 rows orange, 3 rows turquoise, 2 rows orange, 2 rows turquoise.
Next row: cont. in turquoise, rib 2 (1) sts., [m1, rib 1 st.] 0 (1) times * [m1, rib 2 sts.] twice, m1, rib 1 st., rep. from * to last 2 (1) sts., m1, rib to end. 157 (165) sts.
Change to 3¼ mm (no. 10) needles.
Starting with a knit row, cont. in st.st. for 28 rows.

Shape top
1st size: next row: k5, * [k2tog., k6] twice, k2tog., k5, rep. from * to last 14 sts., k2tog., k6, k2tog., k4. 137 sts.
2nd size: next row: k6, * k2tog., k6, rep. from * to last 7 sts., k2tog., k5. 145 sts.
Both sizes: next row: purl.
Next row: k10 (k11), * sl.1(k), k2tog., psso, k20 (k21), rep. from * to last 12 (14) sts., sl.1(k), k2tog., psso, knit to end. 125 (133) sts.
Next row: purl.
Next row: k9 (k10), * sl.1(k), k2tog., psso, k18 (k19), rep. from * to last 11 (13) sts., sl.1(k), k2tog., psso, knit to end. 113 (121) sts.
Next row: purl.
Next row: k8 (k9), * sl.1(k), k2tog., psso, k16 (k17), rep. from

* to last 10 (12) sts., sl.1(k), k2tog., psso, knit to end. 101 (109) sts.
Next row: purl.
Cont. in this way decreasing 12 sts. as before on next and every alt. row until the row k2, * sl.1(k), k2tog., psso, k4 (k3), rep. from * to last 4 (5) sts., sl.1(k), k2tog., psso, knit to end, has been worked. 29 (25) sts.
Next row: purl.
Break off enough yarn to thread through rem. sts. Draw up tightly and fasten off securely.

Make up

Join seam. Cut a circle of cardboard 18 (19) cm / 7 (7½) in in diameter. Insert into beret and press lightly on right side. Remove cardboard. Make one large blackbird (see page 40) and stitch to top of beret. Alternatively, make a black pom-pom (see page 78) for the top. Sew on 2 musical buttons on side of beret.

GLOVES

To make a pair of gloves for this outfit, follow the pattern on page 22, using 25 g of turquoise.

Musical Cushion

MEASUREMENTS

40 cm / 16 in square

MATERIALS

Wool
The numbers in brackets after the colours refer to Rowan Yarn shades in DK lightweight (and 4 ply). Any other double knitting/4 ply can be used provided the tension is the same.

	cushion	birds
turquoise (125)	100 g	
orange (510)	50 g	
black (62)	25 g or oddments	
black 4 ply botany (62)		25 g

Needles and notions
1 pair 4 mm (no. 8) and 1 pair 3¼ mm (no. 10) needles; 1 × 40 cm / 16 in cushion pad; 1 × 28 cm / 11 in zip; 1 musical squeaker

TENSION

24 sts. × 32 rows st.st. on 4 mm (no. 8) needles makes a 10 cm / 4 in square using double knitting

PATTERN

(See also photograph on page 11.)

CUSHION

Using 4 mm (no. 8) needles and turquoise, cast on 84 sts.
Cont. in st.st. following the chart on page 39. Cast off.
Work Swiss darning as indicated on the chart.
Work a plain turquoise underside in st.st. to same size.

MUSICAL CUSHION

Swiss darn words and musical notes

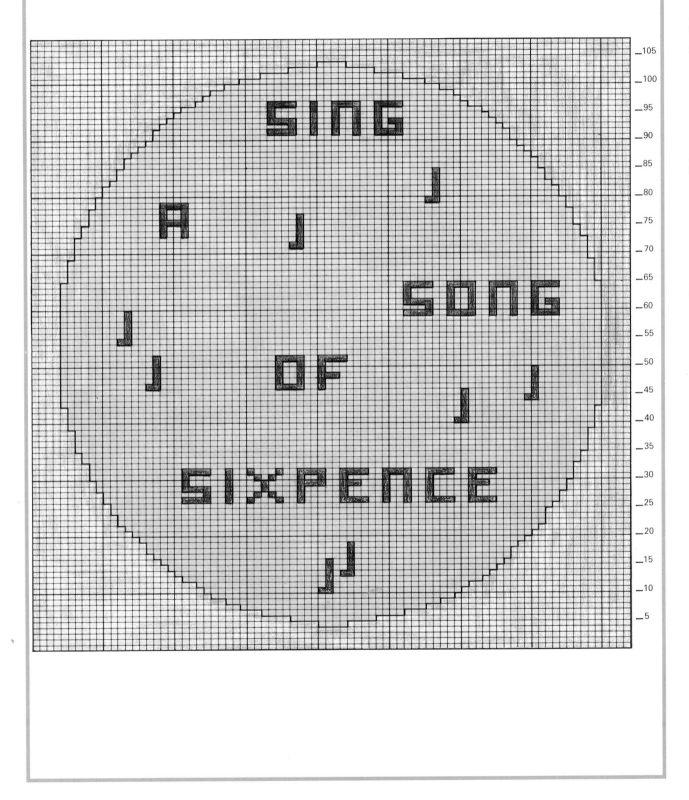

LARGE BLACKBIRDS (make 4)

Body (make 2 pieces)
Using 3¼ mm (no. 10) needles and black, cast on 11 sts following chart (page 41) in garter st.
2nd row: cast on 1 st., knit to end, cast on 2 sts.
3rd row: cast on 2 sts., knit to end, cast on 1 st.
4th row: cast on 1 st., knit to end, cast on 1 st.
5th row: knit to end, cast on 1 st.
6th & 7th rows: rep. 5th row.
8th row: cast on 1 st., knit to end, cast on 1 st.
9th row: knit.
10th row: knit to end, cast on 2 sts.
11th row: knit.
12th row: k2tog., knit to end, cast on 4 sts.
13th row: knit to end, k2tog.
14th row: k2tog., knit to end.
15th row: cast off 4 sts., knit to last 4 sts., k2tog. twice.
16th row: cast off 3 sts., knit to end.
17th row: cast off 3 sts., knit to end.
Cast off.

Wings (make 2 pieces)
1st row: cast on 2 sts.
2nd & 3rd rows: knit.
4th row: knit, casting on 1 st. at each end of row.
5th & 6th rows: knit.
7th row: knit, casting on 1 st. at each end of row.
8th & 9th rows: knit.
10th row: knit, casting on 1 st. at each end of row.
11th to 24th rows: knit.
25th row: knit, casting off 1 st. at each end of row.
26th & 27th rows: knit.
28th row: knit, casting off 1 st. at each end of row.
29th & 30th rows: knit.
31st row: knit, casting off 1 st. at each end of row.
32nd & 33rd row: knit.
Cast off.

Make up
With right sides together, sew up the body pieces leaving top open for stuffing. Turn right way out. Stuff body and stitch up. Make head by gathering sts. round head as indicated on the chart and pull tightly. Stitch eyes in turquoise with a french knot (see page 78). Make beak by sewing 2 french knots with 8 twists each, one on top of the other, using orange. With right sides together, stitch the wings together and turn right way out. Stitch onto bird back along centre of wing. Press beak lightly to form point.
Stitch in zip along 1 side of front and back pieces of cushion. With right sides together, sew up other 3 sides. Lightly press seams. Turn right way out. Stitch one blackbird to each corner of the cushion. Unpick an opening in seam of pad and put in squeaker. Stitch up again. Put pad in cushion and zip up.

Blackbird Mobile

MATERIALS

Wool
The numbers in brackets after the colours refer to Rowan Yarn shades in 4 ply botany. Any other 4 ply can be used provided the tension is the same.

black (62)	25 g
orange (17)	oddments
turquoise (125)	oddments

Needles and notions
1 pair 3¼ (no. 10) needles; kapoc stuffing; glue; 16 gauge piano (music) wire obtained from modelling shops

TENSION

28 sts. × 36 rows st.st. on 3¼ mm (no. 10) needles makes a 10 cm / 4 in square

PATTERN

(See also photograph on page 11.)

Make 5 large blackbirds following the pattern (see left).

Make up
Cut 5 pieces of black yarn 22.5 cm (9 in) long and attach one end to centre back of bird in between wings. Cut the wire into 2 pieces 17.5 cm (7 in) long and 2 pieces 22.5 cm (9 in) long. Hang a bird from either end of one of the 17.5 cm (7 in) long pieces of wire. Tie with a knot, so that the piece of wool measures 10 cm (4 in) from bird to wire. Tie another piece of wool to the centre of this wire, so that the 2 birds on either end balance. Knot the other end to one end of the second 17.5 cm (7 in) piece of wire, so that the wool is 10 cm (4 in) long. Hang another bird 10 cm (4 in) along the second wire and tie another piece of wool to the middle. Slide this along the wire until the single bird balances the other two.
Repeat the last two processes using the two 22.5 cm (9 in) pieces of wire, always keeping 10 cm (4 in) between each wire and bird.
Suspend the whole mobile from a longer piece of wool and attach in chosen place, so that it can swing freely and is out of your child's reach. Adjust all the knots until the balance is perfect. Trim off the ends of the knots and dab a blob of glue to each knot to prevent it from slipping.
Note: Other wire can be used but the above gives an elegant, compact and tangle-free mobile.

BLACKBIRD

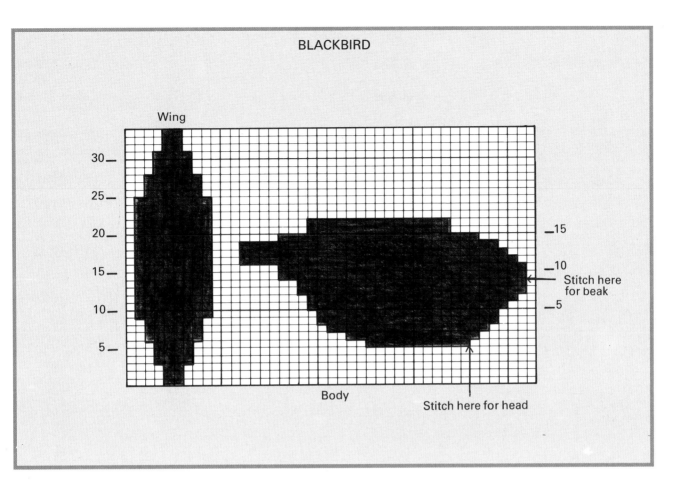

Ring-a-ring o' roses,
A pocket full of posies,
A-tishoo! A-tishoo!
We all fall down.

Ring-a-ring o' Roses

A summer outfit designed for a little girl; both jumper (with short or long sleeves) and skirt are ringed with roses knitted as part of the pattern. Roses also decorate the socks, there is a posy in the skirt pocket and a whole bunch collected into a matching bag. The skirt has an elasticated waist, which will allow for growth. If liked, you could also knit some matching pants to complete the outfit.

MEASUREMENTS

Jumper
Chest: 46 (51, 56) cm / 18 (20, 22) in
Length from centre back of neck: 30 (33, 38) cm / 11¾ (13, 15) in
Sleeve: 7 (9, 10) cm / 2¾ (3½, 4) in

Skirt
Length: 23 (25.5, 28) cm / 9 (10, 11) in
Width at bottom: 62 (67, 70) cm / 24½ (26, 27½) in

Socks
Size: 1–2 years (2–3 years)

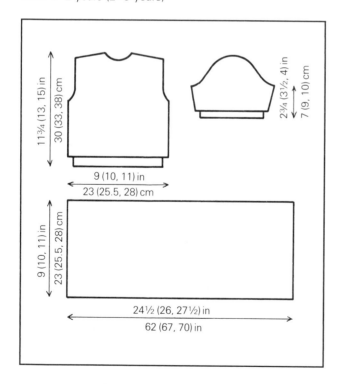

MATERIALS

Wool
The numbers in brackets after the colours refer to Rowan yarn in 4 ply soft cotton – sea breeze. Any other 4 ply cotton can be used provided the tension is the same.

	Jumper	Skirt	Socks
bleached (521) [MS]	100 g (125 g, 150 g)	75 g (100 g, 100 g)	25 g
sugar pink (545)		25 g	
strawberry (546)		25 g	
lilac (544)		25 g	
bluebell (542)		25 g	
pine forest (538)		25 g	

Alternative colourway
A lemon yellow (551) can be used in place of the white as the main shade.

Needles and notions
1 pair 2¾ mm (no. 12), 1 pair 3¼ mm (no. 10) and 1 pair 3 mm (no. 11) needles; 4 small buttons; 25 mm / 1 in wide elastic (for skirt waist)

TENSION

28 sts. × 36 rows st.st. on 3¼ mm (no. 10) needles makes a 10 cm / 4 in square

PATTERN

JUMPER

Back
** Using 2¾ mm (no. 12) needles and MS, cast on 65 (73, 79) sts.
Work in k1, p1, rib until rib measures 4 (4, 5) cm / 1½ (1½, 2) in, increasing evenly in last row to 72 (80, 88) sts.
Change to 3¼ mm (no. 10) needles and, following the chart

below to work the rose motif, work until back measures 20 (23, 25) cm / 8 (9, 10) in, ending with a purl row.

Shape armholes
Cast off 4 sts. at beg. of next 2 rows.
Dec. 1 st. at each end of next and every alt. row until 52 (56, 60) sts. remain. **

Divide for opening
Knit 24 (26, 28) sts., turn and leave rem. sts. on spare needle.
Next row: cast on 4 sts., k4, purl to end. *28 (30, 32) sts.*
Cont. in st.st. until back measures 30 (33, 38) cm / 11¾ (13, 15) in, ending with a WS row.

Shape shoulders
Next row: cast off 4 (5, 4) sts., work to end.
Cast off 4 (5, 4) sts. at beg. of following 2 alt. rows, work to end.
With right side facing, rejoin yarn to rem. 28 (30, 32) sts., knit to end.
Next row: purl to last 4 sts., k4.
Make buttonhole in next row as follows:
k2, yf, k2tog., knit to end.
Complete to match 1st side with 3 more buttonholes on every 4th row.
Cast off.

Front
Following the chart below for rose motif, work as for back from ** to **. Cont. until front measures 27 (30, 36) cm / 10½ (11¾, 14) in.

Divide the neck
Knit 20 (21, 22) sts., turn and leave rem. sts. on spare needle.
Working on these 20 (21, 22) sts. for 1st side, dec. 1 st. at neck edge on every row until 12 (15, 16) sts. remain.
Work straight until front matches back armhole edge.
Shape armholes as for back.
With right side of work facing, rejoin yarn to rem. sts.
Cast off centre 12 (14, 16) sts., knit to end.
Complete to match 1st side.

Sleeves
Using 2¾ mm (no. 12) needles and MS, cast on 45 (49, 53) sts.
Work in k1, p1, rib for 4 (4, 5) cm / 1½ (1½, 2) in, increasing evenly in last row to 50 (54, 58) sts.
Change to 3¼ mm (no. 10) needles and, following the chart on page 47, beg. with a knit row.
Work in st.st. until sleeve measures 7 (9, 10) cm / 2¾ (3½, 4) in, or to length required, ending with a purl row.
Cast off 4 sts. at beg. of next 4 rows.
Dec. 1 st. at each end of next and every alt. row until 38 sts. remain.
Work 1 row.
Dec. 1 st. at each end of every row until 14 sts. remain.
Cast off.

Collar
Using 2¾ mm (no. 12) needles and MS, cast on 55 (59, 63) sts.
Knit 1 row.
Work in k1, p1, rib for 5 (6, 7) cm / 2 (2½, 2¾) in.
Cast off.
Work another piece the same.

Make up
Press work lightly on WS. Sew up shoulder, side and sleeve seams. Set in sleeves. Sew cast off edge of each collar piece round neck, beg. at centre front and ending in centre of back opening. Sew cast on edge of button border neatly behind buttonhole border. Press all seams. Sew on buttons to correspond to buttonholes.
Note: The jumper can be worn with the opening at the front or at the back.

SKIRT

Using 3¼ mm (no. 10) needles and MS, cast on 160 (170, 180) sts.
Knit 4 rows.
Working in st.st., follow the chart on pages 46 and 47 starting at line 1 to work border motif, then cont. in MS until work

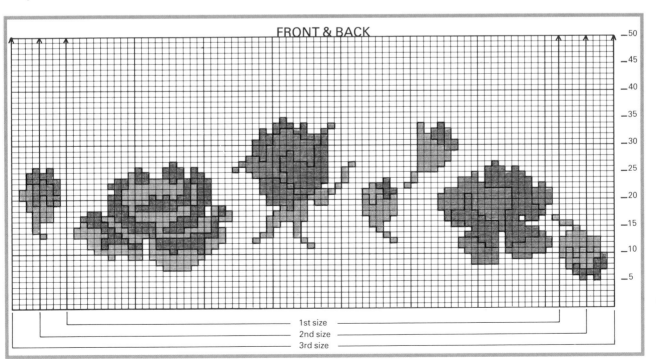

FRONT & BACK

1st size
2nd size
3rd size

measures 20 (23, 25) cm / 8 (9, 10) in or length required.
Change to 2¾ mm (no. 12) needles and work in k1, p1, rib for
6 cm / 2½ in. Cast off in rib.

Pocket

Using 3¼ mm (no. 10) needles and MS, cast on 20 sts.
Work 20 rows in st.st.
Change to 2¾ mm (no. 12) needles and work in k1, p1, rib for
3 cm / 1 in. Cast off in rib.

Make up

Sew up centre back seam and press on WS. Fold over rib and
lightly stitch edge of rib to beg. of rib, leaving a gap for the
elastic. Thread through elastic to fit waist and stitch ends
together. Stitch on pocket. Press. Make up a bunch of 6 roses
and leaves (see page 47) and put in pocket.

SOCKS

Using 3 mm (no. 11) needles and MS, cast on 37 sts.
Work 3 rows in k1, p1, rib, rows on right side having a k1, at
each end.
Change to 3¼ mm (no. 10) needles.
Purl 1 row.

Right side

1st row: k2, * sl.1(p), k3, rep. from * to last 3 sts., sl.1(p), k2.
2nd row: p2, * sl.1(p), p3, rep. from * to last 3 sts., sl.1(p), p2.
3rd row: k4, * sl.1(p), k3, rep. from * to last st., k1.
4th row: p4, * sl.1(p), p3, rep. from * to last st., p1.
5th row: k2, * sl.1(p), k3, rep. from * to last 3 sts., sl.1(p), k2.
6th row: p2, * sl.1(p), p3, rep. from * to last 3 sts., sl.1(p), p2.
7th row: knit.
8th row: purl.
These 8 rows form patt.
Rep. these 8 rows twice (3 times) more, then 1st to 6th rows
again.

Divide for foot

k8, [k2tog.] twice, k13, turn,
Next row: p13, turn,
Starting with a 1st row, work 20 (28) rows in patt. on these sts.
Break yarn, leave sts. on a safety pin.

With right side facing, rejoin to inside edge where 10 sts.
were left and knit up 14 sts. along side of foot, k2tog., k9,
k2tog. from safety pin. Knit up 14 sts. along other side of foot,
then [k2tog.] twice, k8. *59 sts.*
Starting with a purl row, work 7 rows in st.st.

Shape foot

Next row: k2, k2tog., k21, k2tog., k5, k2tog. tbl, k21, k2tog.
tbl, k2.
Next row: purl.
Next row: k2, k2tog., k19, k2tog., k5, k2tog. tbl, k19, k2tog.
tbl, k2.
Next row: purl.
Next row: k2, k2tog., k17, k2tog., k5, k2tog. tbl, k17, k2tog.
tbl, k2.
Next row: purl. Cast off.

Make up

Join leg and foot seams. Stitch a rose and leaf (see page 47)
on outside leg near top.

PANTS

Using white yarn, follow patt. for Little Bo Peep (page 59),
using roses instead of daisies.

Toy Bag and Roses

MEASUREMENTS

Length: 21 cm / 8 in
Width: 15 cm / 6 in

MATERIALS

Wool

The number in brackets after the colour refers to Rowan yarn
in 4 ply soft cotton – sea breeze. Any other 4 ply cotton can be
used provided the tension is the same.

bleached (521) [MS]   50 g
oddments of other colours (see page 44) for motifs and roses

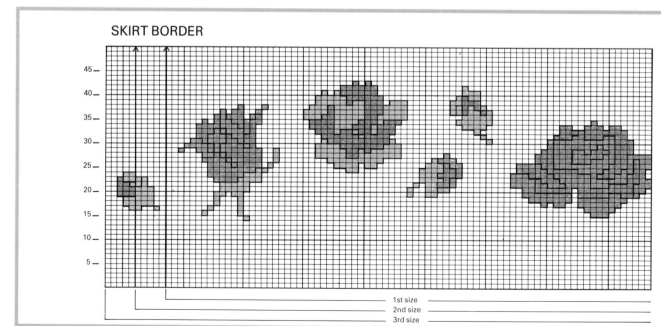

SKIRT BORDER

1st size
2nd size
3rd size

Needles

1 pair 2¾ mm (no. 12) and 1 pair 3¼ mm (no. 10) needles; crochet hook

TENSION

28 sts. × 36 rows st.st. on 3¼ mm (no. 10) needles makes a 10 cm / 4 in square

PATTERN (See also photograph on page 11.)

BAG

Using 3¼ mm (no. 10) needles and MS, cast on 90 sts.
Work 10 rows in st.st.
Following the skirt chart below to work the rose patt., cont. in st.st. until work measures 18 cm / 7 in.
Change to 2¾ mm (no. 12) needles.
Work in k1, p1, rib for 3 cm / 1 in. Cast off in rib.

Make up
Sew sides together. Sew up bottom. Crochet a chain tie for handle 50 cm / 20 in long using double yarn. Thread through beg. of rib. Make a knot in each end about 3 cm / 1 in from end. Fray yarn at ends. Put in a bunch of roses and leaves.

ROSES

Using 2¾ mm (no. 12) needles and a coloured oddment, cast on 31 sts.
Next row: k1, * cast of 4 sts. (1 st. on needle after cast off), rep. from * 5 times. *7 sts. left on needle with a set of 4 cast off sts. between each one*
Knit 2 rows on 7 sts.
Break off enough yarn to thread through rem. sts. Draw up tightly and fasten off securely.

Leaves
Using 2¾ mm (no. 12) needles and an oddment of green, cast on 21 sts.
Next row: k1, * cast off 9 sts. (1 st. on needle after cast off), rep. from * once more. *There should now be 3 sts. on needle.*
Knit 2 rows on these 3 sts.
Break off enough yarn to thread through rem. sts. Draw up tightly and fasten off securely.

Stems
Crochet a chain to required length and fix to the roses.

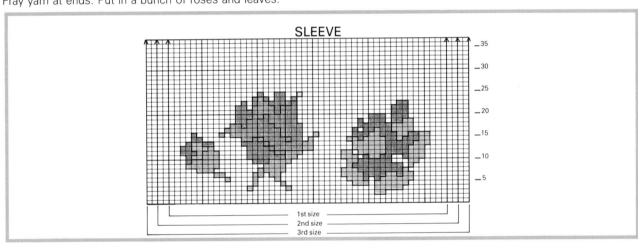

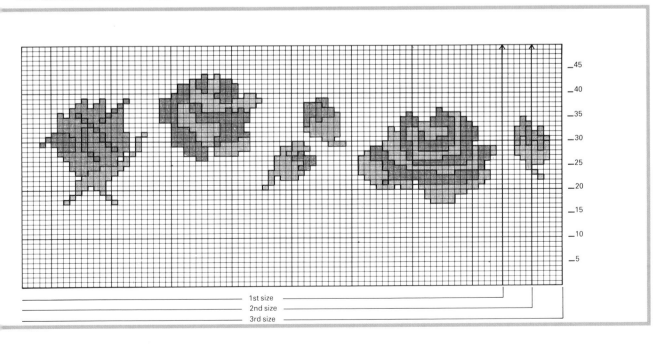

This little piggy went to market,
This little piggy stayed at home,
This little piggy had roast beef,
This little piggy had none,
And this little piggy cried 'Wee, wee, wee'
All the way home.

This Little Piggy

Decorated with four of the little pigs, this outfit includes jacket, shorts and hat, suitable for boys or girls. The fifth little pig – which squeaks, of course – is tucked into the jacket pocket. Five larger versions of this pig can be made into a squeaky toy to play with. They could also be made into a mobile.

MEASUREMENTS

Jacket
Chest: 51 (56, 61) cm / 20 (22, 24) in
Length from centre back of neck: 30 (34, 39) cm / 11¾ (13½, 15¼) in
Sleeve seams: 20 (24, 28) cm / 8 (9½, 11) in

Shorts
Centre waist to crutch (including rib): 23 (24, 25) cm / 9 (9½, 10) in
Inside leg length: 11 (12, 13) cm / 4½ (5, 5½) in

Hat (one size)
Width round head: 42 cm / 16½ in

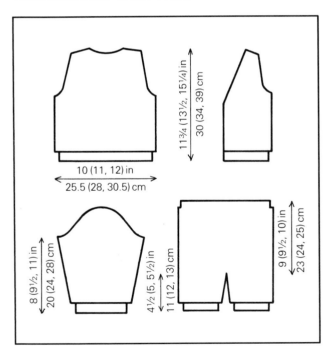

MATERIALS

The numbers in brackets after the colours refer to Rowan Yarn shades in lightweight double knitting. Any other double knitting can be used provided the tension is the same.

Wool

	Jacket	Shorts	Hat
green (606) [MS]	175 g (200 g, 250 g)	100 g (125 g, 175 g)	50 g
red (46)	25 g (or oddments)	oddments	oddments
pink (19)	25 g		
white (110), brown (87)	25 g (or oddments)		

Alternative colourway
Use navy blue (97) in place of the green as the main shade as shown on the contents pages.

Needles and notions
1 pair 3¼ mm (no. 10) and 1 pair 4 mm (no. 8) needles; crochet hook; 4 (5, 6) buttons for jacket; 2 buttons for shorts; scrap of stuffing; squeaker

TENSION

12 sts. × 16 rows st.st. on 4 mm (no. 8) needles measures 5 cm (2 in)

PATTERN

JACKET

Back
Using 3¼ mm (no. 10) needles and MS, cast on 69 (75, 81) sts.
1st row: (right side): k1, * p1, k1, rep. from * to end.
2nd row: p1, * k1, p1, rep. from * to end.
Join in red and work 2 rows in rib, change to MS for 4 (4, 6) rows of rib, then work 2 rib rows in white and 4 (4, 6) rib rows in MS again.
Change to 4 mm (no. 8) needles.
Work in st.st. following the chart on page 52, starting at line 1

and using MS.
Work until back measures 17 (20, 24) cm / 6¾ (8, 9½) in, ending with a purl row.

Shape armholes
Still using MS and continuing in st.st., cast off 3 (3, 4) sts. at beg. of next 2 rows.
Dec. 1 st at each end of next 3 rows, then every alt. row twice. *53 (59, 63) sts. remain*
Work straight until armhole measures 11 (12, 13) cm / 4¼ (4¾, 5) in measured vertically from start of armhole shaping, ending with a purl row.

Shape shoulders
Cast off 5 (6, 6) sts. at beg. of next 4 rows, then 5 (5, 7) sts. at beg. of following 2 rows.
Cast of rem. 23 (25, 25) sts.
Work embroidery and Swiss darning (see page 78) as shown on the chart.

Left front
Pocket lining
Using 4 mm (no. 8) needles and MS, cast on 14 sts.
Continue in st.st. until work measures 5 cm / 2 in, ending on a purl row. Leave sts. on a thread.
Using 3¼ mm (no. 10) needles and MS, cast on 32 (34, 38) sts.
1st row: (right side): * k1, p1, rep. from * to last 2 sts., k2.
2nd row: p2, * k1, p1, rep. from * to end.
Continue as for back to end of rib.
Change to 4 mm (no. 8) needles and still using MS, knit 1 row, decreasing 1 st. at beg. of row for 51 (61) cm / 20 (24) in sizes only. *31 (34, 37) sts.*
Work in st.st. until work measures 10 cm / 4 in ending with a purl row.

Pocket opening
Knit 9 sts., slip 14 sts. onto a thread, knit across 14 sts. left on pocket lining on thread, knit to end.

RIGHT FRONT

Embroider features on pig face and basket handle

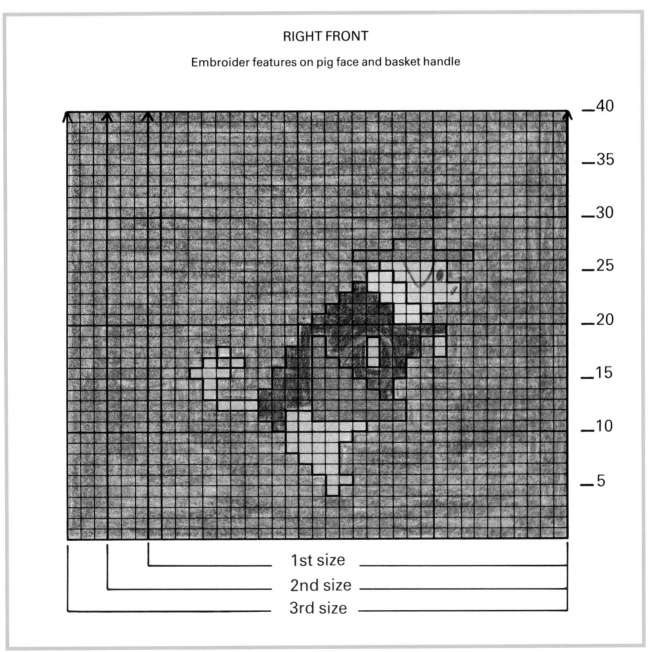

—40

—35

—30

—25

—20

—15

—10

—5

1st size
2nd size
3rd size

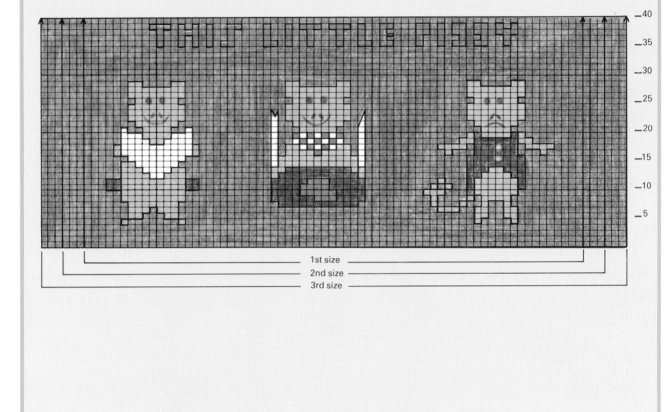

BACK

Embroider features on pig faces
Swiss darn lettering and knife and fork

1st size
2nd size
3rd size

Continue in st.st. until front is 6 rows shorter than back to start of armhole shaping, ending with a purl row.
Tie a marker at beg. of last row.

Shape neck
Dec. 1 st. at end of next and following 4th row. *29 (32, 35) sts.*
Work 1 row straight ending at side edge.

Shape armhole
Cast off 3 (3, 4) sts. at beg. of next row.
Work 1 row.
Dec. 1 st. at neck edge on following 4th row *at the same time* dec. 1 st. at armhole edge on next 3 rows, then every alt. row twice. *19 (22, 24) sts.*
Work 1 row straight.
Keeping armhole edge straight, dec. 1 st. at neck edge on next and every following 4th row, 2 (4, 2) times in all, *17 (18, 22) sts. remain*, then dec. 1 st. at neck edge on every following 6th row, 2 (1, 3) times. *15 (17, 19) sts. remain.*

Work straight until front measures same as back to start of shoulder shaping, ending with a purl row at armhole edge.

Shape shoulder
Cast off 5 (6, 6) sts. at beg. of next and following alt. rows.
Work 1 row.
Cast off rem. 5 (5, 7) sts.

Right front
Using 3¼ mm (no. 10) needles and MS, cast on 32 (34, 37) sts.
1st row: (right side): k2, * p1, k1, rep. from * to end.
2nd row: * p1, k1, rep. from * to last 2 sts., p2.
Continue as for back to end of rib.
Change to 4 mm (no. 8) needles and still using MS, knit 1 row decreasing 1 st. at end of row for 51 (61) cm / 20 (24) in sizes only. *31 (34, 37) sts.*
Work in st.st. following the chart on page 51, starting at line 1 with a purl row, until front is 6 rows shorter than back to start

of armhole shaping, ending with a purl row.
Tie a marker at end of last row.

Shape neck
Dec. 1 st. at beg. of next and following 4th rows.
29 (32, 35) sts. remain.
Work 2 rows straight, ending at side edge.

Shape armhole
Cast off 3 (3, 4) sts. at beg. of next row.
Dec. 1 st. at neck edge on next and following 4th row *at the same time* dec. 1 st. at armhole edge on next 3 rows, then every alt. row twice. *19 (22, 24) sts. remain.*
Work 1 row straight.
Keeping armhole edge straight, dec. 1 st. at neck edge on next and every following 4th row, 2 (4, 2) times in all, *17 (18, 22) sts. remain*, then every following 6th row, 2 (1, 3) times. *15 (17, 19) sts. remain.*
Work straight until front measures same as back to start shoulder shaping, ending with a knit row at armhole edge.

Shape shoulder
Cast off 5 (6, 6) sts. at beg. of next and following alt. rows.
Work 1 row.
Cast off rem. 5 (5, 7) sts.
Work embroidery and Swiss darning as shown on the chart.

Sleeves
Using 3¼ mm (no. 10) needles and MS, cast on 39 (41, 45) sts. and work 14 (14, 18) rows in striped rib as for back.
Change to 4 mm (no. 8) needles and still using MS, work 4 rows in st.st., starting with a knit row.
Inc. 1 st. at each end of next and every following 6th (8th, 9th) row until there are 53 (55, 59) sts.
Work straight until sleeve measures 20 (24, 28) cm / 8 (9½, 11) in, ending with a purl row.

Shape top
Cast off 3 (3, 4) sts. at beg. of next 2 rows.
Dec. 1 st. at each end of next 3 rows, then every alt. row until 29 (29, 27) sts. remain.
Dec. 1 st. at each end of next 3 rows, then cast off 4 sts. at beg. of next 2 rows.
Cast off rem. 15 (15, 13) sts.

Collar

Left half (variations for working right half are given in square brackets)
Using 4 mm (no. 8) needles and MS, cast on 2 sts. and work 2 rows in st.st., starting with a knit row.
Inc. 1 st. at end [beg.] of next and every following 6th (4th, 4th) rows until there are 9 (12, 13) sts.
Work straight until piece measures 15 (16, 17) cm / 6 (6¼, 6¾) in along straight edge, ending with a knit row [purl 1 row more].
Slip sts. onto a stitch holder. Do not break off yarn.
Work right half.

Collar back
Continuing on sts. of right half, cast on 23 (25, 25) sts., turn and purl across sts. of left half. *41 (49, 51) sts.*
Work straight until back collar measures 8 (9, 10) cm / 3 (3½, 4) in, ending with a knit row.
Change to 3¼ mm (no. 10) needles.
Next row: (increase): p5 (p3, p4) * inc. in next st., p5, rep. from * to last 6 (4, 5) sts. inc. in next st., purl to end. *47 (57, 59) sts.*

Tie a marker at each end of row.
Work 2 rows in k1, p1, rib as given for back.
Keeping rib correct, work 1 row in MS, 2 rows red, 4 rows in MS *at the same time* inc. 1 st. at each end of next and following alt. row, then following 4 rows. *59 (69, 71) sts.*
Cast off.

Left front band
Using 3¼ mm (no. 10) needles and MS, with right side facing, start at marker, pick up and knit 42 (52, 64) sts. along front edge.
Work 3 rows in p1, k1, rib. Join red.
Boys: next row: (buttonholes): using red, rib 3 (3, 3), cast off next 2 sts. in rib, rib until there are 9 (9, 9) sts. on right hand needle after casting off 3 (4, 5) times, cast off next 2 sts., rib to end.
Cast on 2 sts. over each cast off sts. on next row.
Girls: using red, work 2 rows in rib.
Boys and girls: Continue in MS for 4 more rows.
Cast off in rib.

Right front band
Pick up and knit sts. as given for left front band but start at lower edge and finish at marker.
Work 3 rows in k1, p1, rib. Join red.
Boys: using red, work 2 rows rib.
Girls: next row: using red, rib 4 (3, 4), cast off next 2 sts. in rib, rib until there are 9 (9, 9) sts. on right needle after casting off 3 (4, 5) times, cast off next 2 sts., rib to end.
Cast on 2 sts over each cast off sts. on next row.
Boys and girls: Continue in MS in rib for 4 more rows.
Cast off in rib.

Collar edging
Using 3¼ mm (no. 8) needles and MS, with right side facing and starting at cast on edge of left half, pick up and knit 65 (71, 75) sts. along side edge of collar marker.
1st row: p1, * k1, p1, rep. from * to end.
Keeping rib correct, work 2 rows in MS, 2 rows in red, 4 rows in MS, *at the same time* inc. 1 st. at back edge of following 2 alt. rows, then next 4 rows.
Using MS, cast off in rib.
Work 2nd side to match but start at marker at back edge of collar on right half.

Pocket border
With right side facing, using 3¼ mm (no. 10) needles and MS and working across 14 sts. left on thread, k3, m1, [k4, m1] twice, k3. *17 sts.*
Continue in rib and work 3 rows in MS, 2 rows in red, 3 rows in MS.
Cast off in rib.

Make up
Sew pocket borders and lining into position. Join shoulders, side and sleeve seams. Insert sleeves. Sew collar to neck edge. Join ends of bands. Sew on buttons to correspond to buttonholes. Put pig into pocket. (Pattern on page 54.)
Note: This can be attached to the pocket with a length of crochet chain but not for an active child, when it could be a safety hazard.

SHORTS

Legs (both the same)
Using 3¼ mm (no. 10) needles and MS, cast on 56 (64, 68) sts.
Work in rib as for back of jacket.

Next row: p3 (p7, p6), m1, [p7 (p7, p8), m1] 7 times, purl to end. *64 (72, 76) sts.*
Change to 4 mm (no. 8) needles and continue in MS in st.st. until work measures 11 (12, 13) cm / 4½ (5, 5½) in or length required, ending on a knit row. Leave sts. on a thread.

Work crutch

Purl across 64 (72, 76) sts. left on thread for one leg and purl across 64 (72, 76) sts. left on thread for other leg. *128 (144, 152) sts.*
Cont. without shaping until crutch measures 19 (20, 22) cm / 7½ (8, 8½) in, ending on a knit row.
Next row: p2 (p1, p5), p2tog., [p2, p2tog., p3, p2tog.] 13 (15, 15) times, p2, p2tog., purl to end. *100 (112, 120) sts.*
Change to 3¼ mm (no. 10) needles and work in rib for 3 cm (1 in), ending on a purl row.
Cast off in rib.

Straps (both the same)

Using 3¼ mm (no. 10) needles and MS, cast on 5 sts.
Work 4 rows in rib.
** Next row: rib 2 sts., cast off 1 st., rib to end.
Next row: rib to last 2 sts., cast on 1 st., rib to end. **
Cont. in rib until work measures 33 cm / 13 in or length required, ending on a purl row.
Work from ** to **.
Work 4 rows in rib.
Cast off in rib.
Fit straps to shorts and sew on buttons on shorts to correspond to buttonholes.

HAT

Using 3¼ mm (no. 10) needles and MS, cast on 96 sts. and work in rib for 1.5 cm / ½ in.
Purl 1 row on WS increasing 6 sts. evenly across row. *102 sts.*
Change to 4 mm (no. 8) needles and cont. in st.st., * 2 rows in MS, 2 rows in red *, rep. from * to * twice more.
Change to garter st. and work 2 rows in MS, 4 rows in red.
Continue in MS in st.st. for 10 rows.
Next row: dec. 8 sts. evenly across hat. *94 sts.*
Rep. these 8 decs. on every following alt. row 9 times, working decs. one above the other until 22 sts. remain.
Next row: p2tog. across row.
Break off yarn leaving enough to thread through rem. sts.
Draw up tightly and fasten off securely.

Ears

Using 4 mm (no. 8) needles and MS, cast on 12 sts. Work in st.st. for 6 rows.
Dec. 1 st. at each end of every alt. row for 8 rows. *4 sts.*
Continue for 3 rows and cast off.
Rep. in MS once. Rep. in red twice.

Make up

For each ear, stitch MS and red pieces tog. with red on the inside. Sew hat seam and attach ears.

PIG FOR POCKET

Body

Using 4 mm (no. 8) needles and pink, cast on 5 sts. Work in st.st.
Knit 1 row.
Next row: inc. 1 st. at each end of row.
Next row: inc. 2 sts. at each end of row.
Work 2 rows in st.st.
Next row: cast on 2 sts., purl to end.

Work 3 rows in st.st.
Next row: cast off 2 sts., purl to last 2 sts., p2tog.
Next row: k2tog., knit to last 2 sts., k2tog.
Next row: p2tog., purl to last 2 sts., p2tog.
Next row: k2tog., knit to last 2 sts., k2tog.
Purl 1 row.
Next row: inc. 1 st. at each end of row.
Rep. last row.
Next row: inc. 1 st. at each end of row.
Next row: cast on 2 sts., purl to last st., inc. in last st.
Work 3 rows in st.st.
Next row: cast off 2 sts., purl to end.
Work 2 rows in st.st.
Next row: dec. 2 sts. at each end of row.
Next row: dec 1 st. at each end of row.
Knit 1 row.
Cast off.

Ears (make 2 pieces)

Cast on 5 sts.
Work 2 rows in st.st.
Next row: dec. 1 st. at each end of row.
Next row: k3tog. Thread yarn through last st. and fasten off neatly.

Legs (make 4 pieces)

Cast on 6 sts.
Work 2 rows in st.st.
Next row: k2tog. at each end of row.
Work 2 rows in st.st.
Cast off.

Snout

Cast on 3 sts.
Work 2 rows in st.st.
Cast off.

Tail

Crochet a chain (see page 78) 7.5 cm (3 in) long.

Make up

Stitch up body and snout, leaving hole at base for stuffing and squeaker, insert, then stitch up completely. Attach ears. Sew up legs and attach to body. Attach tail. Embroider eyes using French knots (see page 78).

5 Toy Squeaky Pigs or Mobile

MEASUREMENTS

Height: approx. 9 cm / 3½ in

MATERIALS

Wool

The number in brackets after the colour refers to the Rowan Yarn shade in lightweight double knitting. Any other double knitting can be used provided the tension is the same.

pink (19) 50 g
scrap of brown for embroidery

Needles and notions

1 pair 4 mm (no. 8) needles; pipe cleaners; kapoc stuffing; red polka dot ribbon for bows; 5 squeakers

TENSION

24 sts. × 32 rows on 4 mm (no. 8) needles makes a 10 cm / 4 in square

PATTERN

Make 5 pigs.
(See also photograph on page 11.)

Body (make 1 piece)

Using 4 mm (no. 8) needles and pink, cast on 10 sts. Work in st.st. throughout.
Knit 1 row.
Next row: inc. 1 st. at each end of row.
Rep. last row.
Next row: inc. 2 sts. at each end of row.
Rep. last row.
Work 4 rows in st.st.
Next row: cast on 4 sts., purl to end. (snout) *26 sts.*
Work 5 rows in st.st.
Next row: cast off 4 sts., purl to last 2 sts., p2tog.
Next row: k2tog., knit to last 2 sts., k2tog.
Next row: purl to last 2 sts., p2tog.
Next row: k2tog., knit to end.
Next row: p2tog., purl to last 2 sts., p2tog.
Next row: k2tog., knit to last 2 sts., k2tog.
Next row: purl.
Next row: inc. 1 st. at each end of row.
Rep. last row.
Next row: inc. 1 st., knit to end.
Next row: purl to last st., inc. 1 st.
Next row: inc. 1 st. at each end of row.
Next row: cast on 4 sts., purl to last st., inc. in last st.
Work 5 rows in st.st.
Next row: cast off 4 sts., purl to end.
Work 4 rows in st.st.
Next row: dec. 2 sts. at each end of row.
Rep. last row.
Next row: dec. 1 st. at each end of row.
Rep. last row.
Next row: knit.
Cast off.

Ears (make 2 pieces)

Cast on 7 sts.
Beginning with a knit row, work 2 rows in st.st.
Next row: dec. 1 st. at each end of row.
Rep. last row.
Next row: k3tog.
Thread yarn through last st. Break off yarn and fasten off neatly.

Legs (make 4 pieces)

Cast on 10 sts.
Beginning with a knit row, work 4 rows in st.st.
Next row: k2tog., knit to last 2 sts., k2tog.
Work 2 rows in st.st.
Next row: k2tog., knit to last 2 sts., k2tog.
Work 2 rows in st.st.
Cast off.

Snout

Cast on 4 sts.
Work 3 rows in st.st.
Cast off.

Tail

Cast on 4 sts. and work in st.st. until work measures 10 cm / 4 in. Cast off. With right sides together, stitch up seam and turn right way out. Put pipe cleaner inside and curl up like a pig's tail.
Note: If you are worried about the safety aspect of the pipe cleaner, omit, curl up the tail and stitch in position.

Make up

Stitch up body and snout leaving hole at base for stuffing and squeaker. Insert, then stitch up. Attach ears. With right sides together, sew up legs, then turn right way out. Stuff and attach to body. Attach tail. Embroider features on face and trotters. Tie ribbon round tails and make into bows. If you like the pigs' tails can be joined to the snouts to form a line of 5 pigs.

PIG MOBILE

Make 5 pigs following the above instructions. To assemble the mobile, follow the instructions for the blackbird mobile on page 40.

Little Bo-peep has lost her sheep,
  And doesn't know where to find them;
Leave them alone, and they'll come home,
  Bringing their tails behind them.

Little Bo-peep

In two sizes for little girls, this outfit has a dress with a full, gathered skirt – decorated with Bo-peep and the sheep she is searching for – together with matching pants and booties. There is also a soft toy lamb to play hide and seek with.

MEASUREMENTS

Dress
Chest: 46 (56) cm / 18 (22) in
Length from centre back of neck: 33 (38) cm / 13 (15) in
Sleeve: 9 (11) cm / 3½ (4½) in

Pants
Length from centre back of waist to crutch: 21.5 (24) cm / 8½ (9½) in

Booties
Length of foot seam: 10 (11 cm) / 4 (4½) in

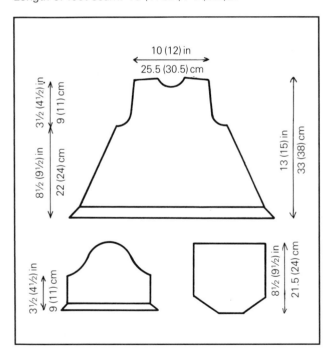

MATERIALS

Wool
The numbers in brackets after the colours refer to Rowan Yarns in cabled mercerised cotton and knobbly cotton for the white. Any other 4 ply cotton can be used provided the tension is the same.

	Dress	Pants	Booties
hydro (323) [MS]	225 g (250 g)	75 g	25 g
bleached (white) (302)	oddments	oddments	oddments
washed straw (305),			
livid (red) (321),			
lichen (327),	oddments		
silver lining (316),			
pale pink (328)			
knobbly cotton white (560) 25 g			

Alternative colourway
Use pastel peach (313) or old rose (312) in place of the main shade.

Needles and notions
1 pair 3¼ mm (no. 10) and 1 pair 2¼ mm (no. 13) needles; 3 metres / 3 yards × 5 mm / ¼ in red ribbon; 4 buttons; elastic for waist (pants)

TENSION

30 sts. × 38 rows st.st. on 3¼ mm (no. 10) needles makes a 10 cm / 4 in square

PATTERN

DRESS

Back
Using 3¼ mm (no. 10) needles and MS, cast on 297 (361) sts.
Work 2 rows in garter st.
Change to st.st. and cont. until work measures 4 cm / 1½ in, ending on a WS row.
Next row: k1, * k2tog., rep. from * to end. *149 (181) sts.*
Work 3 rows in garter st.

Following the chart for the back on pages 60 and 61, starting at line 1, cont. in st.st. until work measures 22 (24) cm / 8½ (9½) in or until length required, ending with a WS row.

Decrease for bodice
Next row: k1, * k2tog., rep. from * to end. *75 (91) sts.*
Work 3 rows in garter st. ***
Next row: k2, * yf, k2tog., rep. from * to last st., k1.
Work 3 rows in garter st.
Cont. as follows in st.st.:

Shape armholes and divide for back opening
Cast off 5 sts., k29 (k37), turn,
Working on these 30 (38) sts., proceed as follows:
Next row: purl.
** Dec. 1 st at armhole edge in every row to 24 (32) sts.
Cont. without shaping until armhole measures 9 (11) cm / 3½ (4½) in, ending on a WS row. **

Shape shoulder and back of neck
Next row: cast off 13 (19) sts., knit to end. Leave rem. 11 (13) sts. on a thread.
With right side facing, work on rem. 40 (48) sts. and proceed as follows:
Next row: slip 5 sts. onto a thread, knit to end.
Next row: cast off 5 sts., purl to end.
Work rem. 30 (38) sts. from ** to **.
Knit and slip 11 (13) sts. onto a thread, cast off rem. 13 (19) sts.

Front
Work exactly as given for back but following the chart for the front on pages 60 and 61, until *** is reached.
Working in st.st., proceed as follows:
Shape armholes (follow the chart for the bodice on page 61, starting at line 1 and working lambs in garter st. using knobbly cotton)
Cast off 5 sts. at beg. of next 2 rows.
Dec. 1 st. at each end of every row to 53 (69) sts.
Work 16 rows without shaping.

Shape neck
Knit 22 (28) sts., turn,
Working on these 22 (28) sts., proceed as follows:
Dec 1 st. at neck edge in every row until 13 (19) sts. remain.
Cont. without shaping until armhole measures same as back.
Cast off. **
With right side facing, work on rem. 31 (41) sts. and proceed as follows:
Slip 9 (13) sts. onto a thread, knit to end.
Work rem. 22 (28) sts. from ** to **.

Sleeves
Using 3¼ mm (no. 10) needles and MS, cast on 65 (77) sts.
Work 2 rows in garter st.
Work 8 rows in st.st.
Next row: k3, * k2tog., k1, rep. from * to last 2 sts., k2. *45 (53) sts.*
Next row: knit.
Next row: k1, * yf, k2tog., rep. from * to last st., k1.
Next row: knit.
Next row: [k4, m1] 19 (23) times, knit to end. *65 (77) sts.*
Next row: purl.
Working in st.st., cont. until work measures 9 (11) cm / 3½ (4½) in, ending on a WS row.

Shape top
Cast on 5 sts. at beg. of next 2 rows.
Work 3 rows without shaping.

** Work 6 (5) rows, decreasing 1 st. at each end of 1st and 4th row.
Rep. from ** to 39 sts. ending with a WS row.
Next row: [k3tog.] 3 times, take 1st 2 sts. over 3rd st. on right hand needle, * [k3tog.] twice, take 1st 2 sts. over 3rd st. on right hand needle, rep. from * to end. Fasten off.

Borders
Right back border
With right side facing, using 2¾ mm (no. 12) needles and MS, work across 5 sts. left on thread as follows:
k2, [m1, k1] twice, k1. *7 sts.*
Work 3 rows in garter st.
Next row: k2, cast off 2 sts., knit to end.
Next row: k3, cast off 2 sts., knit to end.
Cont. in garter st., making another 3 buttonholes as before on 13th (14th) and 17th (18th) rows from 1st buttonhole.
Work 3 rows. **
Next row: cast off 3 sts., knit to end, leave rem. 4 sts. on a thread.

Left back border
Using 2¾ mm (no. 12) needles, cast on 7 sts.
Work to match right back border omitting buttonholes until **.
Next row: knit and slip 4 sts. on a thread, cast off rem. 3 sts.

Make up and neckband
Sew up shoulder seams. With right side facing, using 2¾ mm (no. 12) needles, pick up and knit 4 sts. on left on thread for left back border, 11 (13) sts. left on thread on left side of back neck, 20 sts. down left side of front neck, 9 (13) sts. on thread at front neck, 20 sts. up right side of front neck, 11 (13) sts. left on thread at right side of back neck and 4 sts. left on thread for right back border. *79 (87) sts.*
** Knit 1 row.
Work 3 rows in st.st.
Next row: p1, * yrn, p2tog., rep. from * to end.
Work 3 rows in st.st.
Cast off. **
Sew sleeve in crown position easing in fullness. Sew up rem. seams. Sew borders in position. Sew on buttons to correspond to buttonholes.
To form picot edge on neckband, fold last 3 rows of st.st. onto wrong side and sew loosely in position.

Embroidery
Chain st. ribbon from staff on front of dress. Sew french knots for flowers on hat. Sew french knots for eyes on lambs on bodice. Following the charts for front and back of dress on pages 60 and 61, sew on the flowers using daisy stitch for the white petals and a french knot for the yellow centres.
Thread ribbon through eyelet holes on bodice and sleeves.

PANTS

Worked in one piece starting at back waist edge
Using 2¾ mm (no. 12) needles and MS, cast on 69 (83) sts.
Work 14 rows in k1, p1, rib.
Change to 3¼ mm (no. 10) needles and st.st.
Work 2 rows in st.st.

Shape back
k62 (k76), turn,
sl.1, p54 (p68), turn,
sl.1, k47 (k61), turn,
sl.1, p40 (p54), turn,
sl.1, k33 (k47), turn,

DRESS FRONT
Lamb in garter st.
Ribbon from staff in chain st.
Flowers on hat in french knots
Flowers worked in chain st. with french knot in centre

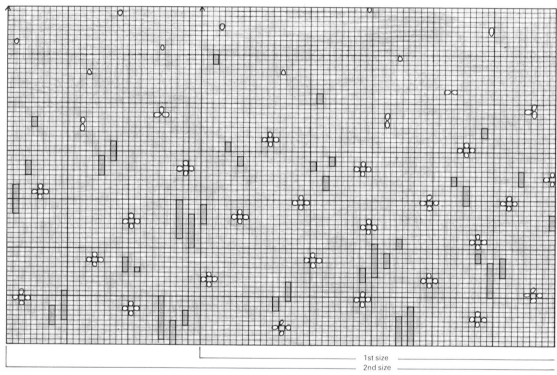

1st size
2nd size

DRESS BACK

1st size
2nd size

DRESS BODICE FRONT Lambs in garter st.

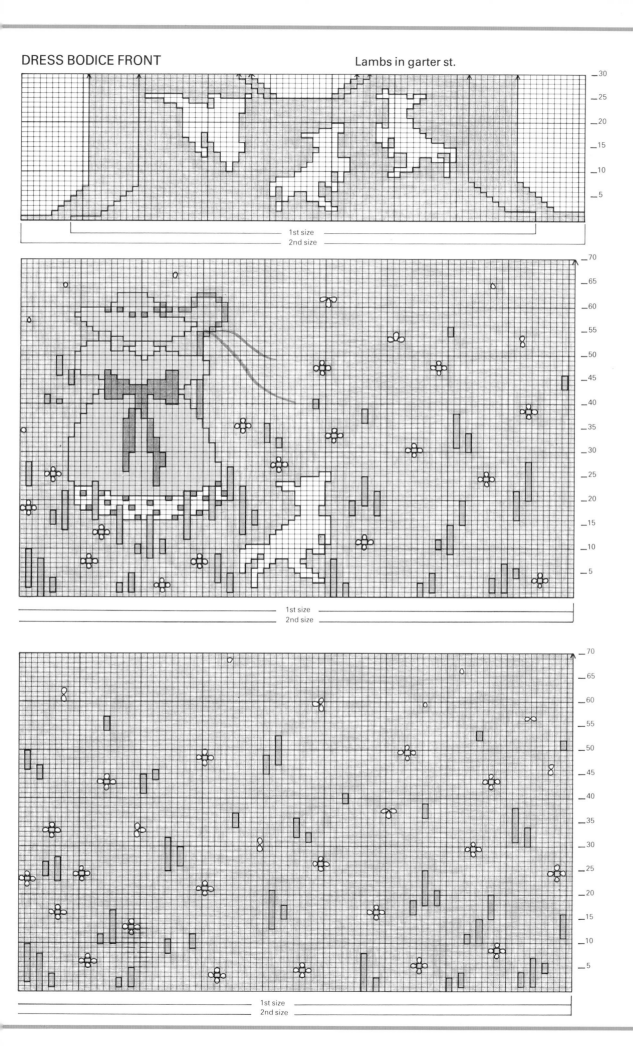

1st size
2nd size

1st size
2nd size

1st size
2nd size

sl.1, p26 (p40), turn,
sl.1, k19 (k33), turn,
sl.1, p12 (p26), turn,
sl.1, knit to end of row.
Purl across all sts.
Cont. in st.st., inc. 1 st. at each end of the needle on the 5th
and every foll. 10th row until 75 (89) sts. are on needle.
Work 5 (9) rows.

Shape leg opening
Dec. 1 st. at each end of needle on the next and every
following alt. row until 65 (81) sts. remain, then each end of
every row until 23 (27) sts. remain.
Work 10 (14) rows.
Inc. 1 st. at each end of the needle on the next and every
following alt. row until 33 (37) sts. are on needle, then at each
end of every row until 51 (55) sts. are on needle.
Cast on 12 (17) sts. at beg. of next 2 rows. *75 (89) sts.*
Dec. 1 st. at each end of the needle on 5th (9th) and every
following 10th row until 69 (83) sts. remain.
Work 9 rows.
Change to 2¾ mm (no. 12) needles.
Work 14 rows in k1, p1, rib. Cast off in rib.

Make up
Legbands
With right side of work facing, using 2¾ mm (no. 12) needles,
pick up and knit 71 (83) sts. evenly around leg opening.
Starting on a 2nd row, work 15 rows in k1, p1, rib.
Cast off loosely in rib. Join side seams by backstitching,
omitting rib. Join rib by top sewing. Fold waist rib in half onto
wrong side and slip stitch loosely in position, leaving a small
opening to insert elastic. Insert elastic to fit waist and stitch to
secure. Fold leg bands in half on wrong side and slip stitch
loosely into position. Make 2 daisies and stitch onto each side
rib of leg opening.

BOOTIES
Using 3¼ mm (no. 10) needles and MS, cast on 37 (45) sts.
Work 3 rows in st.st.
Next row: p1, * yrn, p2tog., rep. from * to end of row.
Work 3 rows in st.st.
Work 3 rows in garter st.

Shape instep
k25 (k30), turn,
p13 (p15), turn,
Working on these 13 (15) sts. only, proceed as follows:
1st row: k3 (k4), [yf, sl.1, k2tog., psso, yf, k1] twice, k2 (k3).
2nd row: purl.
3rd row: k4 (k5), yf, sl.1, k1, psso, k1, k2tog. tbl, yf, k4 (k5).
4th row: purl.
Rep. 1st to 4th rows twice. Break yarn.
With right side facing, rejoin yarn to instep end of first 12 sts.,
pick up and knit 10 sts. evenly along right side of instep, knit
across 13 (15) sts., pick up and knit 10 sts. evenly along side of
instep, knit across rem. 12 (15) sts. *57 (65) sts.*
Work 15 rows in garter st.

Shape foot
1st row: k1, k2tog., k19 (k22), k2tog. tbl, k9 (k11), k2tog., k19
(k22), k2tog. tbl, k1.
2nd row: knit.
3rd row: k1, k2tog., k18 (k21), k2tog. tbl, k7 (k9), k2tog., k18
(k21), k2tog. tbl, k1.
4th row: knit. Cast off.

Make up
Sew up leg and foot seams. To form picot edge, fold back 3
rows of st.st. on wrong side and sew loosely into position.
Thread ribbon through ankles. Stitch a daisy (see below) onto
each foot at front.

DAISY (Make 6: 2 (pants); 2 (booties); 2 (lamb)

Using 3¼ mm (no. 10) needles and white, cast on 6 sts.
Knit 3 rows.
Next row: inc. 1 st. at each end.
Next row: knit.
Rep. last 2 rows until 12 sts.
Knit 3 rows.
Next row: dec. 1 st. at each end.
Next row: knit.
Rep. last 2 rows until 6 sts. remain.
Knit 3 rows.
Cast off.
With yellow yarn, stitch centre, gathering in daisy and making
centre knot.

Toy Lamb

MEASUREMENTS

Height: 25 cm / 10 in
Length: 30 cm / 12 in

MATERIALS

Wool
The number in brackets after the colour refers to a Rowan
Yarns shade in knobbly cotton/salad days. Any other 4 ply
cotton can be used provided the tension is the same.

white (560)   100 g
oddment of black for features
oddment of green for crochet chain

Needles and notions
1 pair 3¾ mm (no. 9) needles; crochet hook; kapoc stuffing; 1
bell (optional); 70 cm / 26 in × 5 mm / ¼ in red ribbon

TENSION

30 sts. × 40 rows st.st. on 3¾ mm (no. 9) needles makes a
10 cm / 4 in square

PATTERN

(See also photograph on page 11.)

Body
** Using 3¾ mm (no. 9) needles, cast on 12 sts. Work in
garter st.
*** **1st row:** knit.
2nd row: inc. 1 st. at each end.
3rd row: inc. in 1st st., knit to end.
4th row: inc. 1 st. at each end.
5th row: knit.
6th row: k2tog., knit to end.
Knit 3 rows.
10th row: k2tog., knit to end.
Knit 3 rows.
14th row: k2tog., knit to end.

15th row: knit.
16th row: k2tog., knit to end.
17th row: knit.
18th row: k2tog., knit to end. *12 sts.* ***
19th row: knit.
Knit 8 rows.
Next row: inc. 1 st. at each end.
Rep. last 9 rows.
Next row: inc. 1 st., knit to end.
Next row: knit to last st., inc. in last st.
Next row: inc. 1 st., knit to end. *19 sts.*
Next row: cast off 5 sts., knit to last st., inc. in last st.
Next row: inc. in 1st st., knit to end.
Next row: knit to last st, inc. in last st.
Next row: inc. 1 st. at each end.
Next row: knit to last st., inc. in last st.
Next row: inc. in 1st st., knit to end.
Next row: knit to last st., inc. in last st. *22 sts.*
Break yarn.
On same needle, cast on 12 sts.
Work from *** to ***.
Next row: cast on 3 sts., knit to end.
Next row: knit.
Next row: cast on 4 sts., knit to end.
Next row: knit.
Next row: cast on 2 sts., knit to end.
Next row: knit.
Next row: inc. 1 st. at each end.
Next row: knit.
Next row: inc. in 1st st., knit to end.
Next row: knit to last st., inc. in last st.
Rep. last 2 rows twice. *29 sts.*
Next row: knit.
Knit across 22 sts. of 1st leg. *51 sts.*
Next row: knit.
Next row: inc. in 1st st., knit to end.
Next row: inc. in 1st st., knit to end.
Knit 2 rows. *53 sts.* **
Next row: knit to last 2 sts., k2tog.
Knit 3 rows.
Next row: inc. in 1st st., knit to end.
Rep. last 4 rows once. *54 sts.*
Next row: k2tog., knit to end.
Knit 3 rows.
Rep. last 4 rows 3 times. *50 sts.*
Cast off.
Work another piece the same.

Underbody
Work as for body from ** to **. Cast off.
Work another piece the same.

Pads (make 4)
Cast on 5 sts.
Knit 1 row.
Next row: inc. 1 st. at each end.
Rep. last row.
Knit 7 rows.
Next row: k2tog., knit to last 2 sts., k2tog.
Rep. last row.
Cast off.

Make up
Join cast off edges of underbody together. Join cast off edges of main body, leaving about 5 cm / 2 in open at neck edge for head. Join body and underbody, sewing up front and back seams, leaving leg ends open. Sew pads round openings, stuff firmly shaping legs and feet.

Head
Cast on 17 sts.
Knit 6 rows.
Next row: inc. in 1st st., knit to end.
Next row: knit to last st., inc. in last st.
Next row: cast on 7 sts., knit to end.
Knit 5 rows.
Next row: knit to last st., inc. in last st. *27 sts.*
Knit 7 rows.
Next row: k2tog., knit to end.
Next row: knit to last 2 sts., k2tog.
Rep. last 2 rows 3 times. *19 sts.*
Next row: knit.
Next row: knit to last 2 sts., k2tog.
Next row: k2tog., knit to last 2 sts., k2tog.
Next row: knit.
Rep. last 2 rows twice. *12 sts.*
Cast off.
Work another piece the same.

Head gusset
Start at nose. Cast on 2 sts.
1st row: knit.
2nd row: inc 1 st. at each end.
Rep. last 2 rows 4 times. *12 sts.*
Knit 2 rows.
Next row: inc. 1 st. at each end.
Rep. last 3 rows 4 times. *22 sts.*
Knit 16 rows.
Next row: k2tog., knit to last 2 sts., k2tog.
Knit 3 rows.
Next row: k2tog., knit to last 2 sts., k2tog.
Rep. last 4 rows 6 times. *6 sts.*
Cast off.
Sew gusset between halves of head starting at nose – cast on edge of gusset comes just above nose tip – join main head pieces together for lower part of face and underchin, leaving neck end open. Stuff firmly and sew open end of neck round opening of body.
Embroider features.

Ears
Cast on 3 sts.
Knit 2 rows.
Next row: inc. in 1st st., knit to last st., inc. in last st.
Rep. last 3 rows. *17 sts.*
Knit 10 rows.
Cast off.
Work another piece the same.
Fold wide edges into centre and stitch onto head.

Tail
Cast on 15 sts.
Knit 10 rows.
Next row: inc. 1 st. at each end.
Rep. last 11 rows twice. *21 sts.*
Knit 42 rows.
Next row: k2tog., knit to last 2 sts., k2tog.
Rep. last row until 3 sts. remain.
Cast off.
Fold strip in half lengthways and join seam leaving cast on edge open. Stuff and sew open end to body.
Tie ribbon round neck. Using oddment of green, make a crochet chain (see page 78) 10 cm / 4 in long and attach a daisy (see page 62) at each end. Stitch with bell (if using) onto ribbon on underside of neck.

Wee Willie Winkie runs through the town,
Upstairs and downstairs in his night-gown,
Knocking at the window, crying through the lock,
Are the children all in bed, for now it's eight o'clock?

Wee Willie Winkie

A matching bedtime outfit of nightshirt, slippers and nightcap and including a hot water bottle cover featuring Wee Willie Winkie. He appears again as a toy to make a cuddly bedtime companion. A shorter version of the nightshirt would make a bright summer jumper.

MEASUREMENTS

Nightshirt
Chest: 51 (56, 61) cm / 20 (22, 24) in
Length from centre back of neck: 58 (65, 70) cm / 23 (25, 28) in
Sleeve: 18 (19, 20) cm / 7 (7½, 8) in

Slippers (one size)
Length of foot: 10 cm / 4 in

Nightcap (one size)
Width round head: 53 cm / 21 in

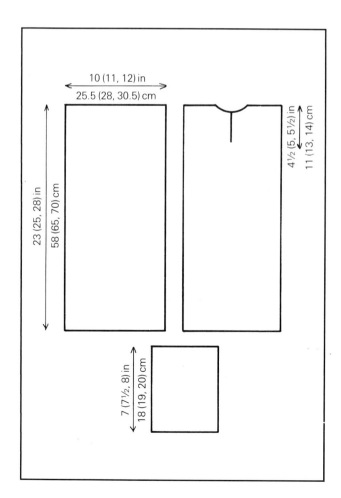

10 (11, 12) in
25.5 (28, 30.5) cm

23 (25, 28) in
58 (65, 70) cm

4½ (5, 5½) in
11 (13, 14) cm

7 (7½, 8) in
18 (19, 20) cm

MATERIALS

Wool
The numbers in brackets after the colours refer to Rowan Yarns soft cotton sea breeze. Any other cotton 4 ply can be used provided the tension is the same.

	Nightshirt	Slippers	Nightcap
bleached (521)	50 g (75 g, 75 g)		
blue polka (530)	50 g (75 g, 75 g)	25 g	50 g
oddments of contrasting yarn for features (slippers)			

Alternative colourway
Bermuda (539) — a pale turquoise can be used in place of the blue polka.

Needles and notions
1 pair 2¾ mm (no. 12), 1 pair 3¼ mm (no. 10) and 1 pair 3 mm (no. 11) needles; 2 (3, 3) buttons (nightshirt); 1 bell (nightcap)

TENSION

28 sts. × 36 rows st.st. on 3¼ mm (no. 10) needles makes a 10 cm / 4 in square

PATTERN

NIGHTSHIRT

Back
Using 3¼ mm (no. 10) needles and cream, cast on 71 (75, 83) sts.
Work in k2, p2, rib for 5 cm / 2 in, working in stripes (2 rows cream, 1 row blue, 2 rows cream, 1 row blue, etc.) and ending on RS row.
Change to st.st. and continue in stripe patt. for 58 (65, 70) cm / 23 (25, 28) in. If knitting the shortened version, continue in stripe patt. for 38 (45, 50) cm / 15 (17, 20) in.
Cast off.

Front
Work exactly as back until work measures 11 (13, 14) cm / 4½ (5, 5½) in less than back ending on RS row.
Next row: (divide for opening): continuing sequence of stripes, work in st.st. for 32 (34, 38) sts., cast off 7 sts., st.st. to end.

Working on 1st 32 (34, 38) sts. and keeping sequence of stripes, proceed as follows:

** cont. without shaping until work measures 5 cm / 2 in less than back, ending at neck edge.

Shape neck

Cast off 3 (3, 4) sts., st.st. to end. **
*** Dec. 1 st. at neck edge in next and every alt. row to 23 (25, 28) sts. Cont. without shaping until work measures same as back.
Cast off. ***
With right side facing, work rem. 32 (34, 38) sts. from ** to **.
Next row: st.st. to end.
Work rem. 29 (31, 34) sts. from *** to ***.

Sleeves

Using 3¼ mm (no. 10) needles and cream, cast on 55 (59, 67) sts.
Cont. in st.st. in stripe patt. (2 rows cream, 1 row blue) until work measures 18 (19, 20) cm / 7 (7½, 8) in or length required.
Cast off.

Buttonhole border

With right side facing, using 2¾ mm (no. 12) needles and cream, pick up and knit 23 (29, 33) sts. along left front edge.
Cont. in k2, p2, rib for 4 rows.
Next row: rib 3 sts., cast off 2 sts., [rib 11 (7, 9) sts., cast off 2 sts.] once (twice, twice), rib to end.
Next row: rib 4 sts., cast on 2 sts., [rib 12 (8, 10) sts., cast on 2 sts.] once (twice, twice), rib to end.
Work 4 rows in rib.
Cast off in rib.

Button border

Work to match buttonhole border omitting buttonholes.

Make up and neckband

Sew up shoulder seams. Press. With right side facing, using 2¾ mm (no. 12) needles and cream, pick up and knit 10 sts. across button border, 21 (23, 24) sts. up right side of neck, 29 (29, 31) sts. evenly across cast off sts. at back of neck, 21 (23, 24) sts. down left side of neck and 10 sts. across other border. 91 (95, 99) sts.
Work 4 rows rib.
Next row: rib 4 sts., cast off 2 sts., rib to end.
Next row: rib to last 4 sts., cast on 2 sts., rib to end.
Work 4 rows in rib.
Cast off in rib.
Place centre of sleeve top at shoulder seam. Sew evenly in position along back and front edges. Sew up rem. seams. Press.
Sew on buttons to correspond to buttonholes.

SLIPPERS

Using 3 mm (no. 11) needles and blue, cast on 37 sts. and work 20 rows in k1, p1, rib, rows on right side having a k1 at each end.
Change to 3¼ mm (no. 10) needles and divide for foot.
Next row: k8, [k2tog.] twice, k13, turn,
Next row: p13 turn,
Starting with a knit row, work 20 rows in st.st. Break off yarn, leaving sts. on a safety pin.
With right side facing, rejoin yarn to inside edge where 10 sts. were left and knit up 14 sts. along side of foot, k2tog., k9, k2tog. from safety pin, knit up 14 sts along other side of foot, then [k2tog.] twice, k8. 59 sts.
Starting with a purl row, work 7 rows in st.st.

Shape foot

1st row: k2, k2tog., k21, k2tog., k5, k2tog. tbl, k21, k2tog. tbl, k2.
2nd row: purl.
3rd row: k2, k2tog., k19, k2tog., k5, k2tog. tbl, k19, k2tog. tbl, k2.
4th row: purl.
5th row: k2, k2tog., k17, k2tog., k5, k2tog. tbl, k17, k2tog. tbl, k2.
6th row: purl.
Cast off.

Make up

Join leg and foot seams. Embroider features.

NIGHTCAP

Using 3¼ mm (no. 10) needles and blue, cast on 136 sts.
Starting with a knit row, work 22 rows in st.st.
Next row: [k2tog., k13, k2tog. tbl] 8 times. 120 sts.
Work 10 rows st.st.
Next row: [k2tog., k11, k2tog. tbl] 8 times. 104 sts.
Work 10 rows st.st.
Cont. to dec. in this manner, working 2 sts. less between decreases until 24 sts. remain.
Work 10 rows st.st.
Next row: [k3tog.] 8 times. 8 sts.
Break off yarn, leaving enough to thread through remaining sts. Draw up tightly and fasten off securely.

Make up

Sew up seam. Fold hem onto wrong side and slip stitch into position. Sew bell on end.
Note: If you prefer not to have the bell, a blue pom-pom or tassel (see page 78) could be attached instead.

Toy Wee Willie Winkie

MEASUREMENTS

Height: 35 cm / 14 in

MATERIALS

Wool

The numbers in brackets after the colours refer to Rowan Yarns handknit double knitting cotton and soft cotton sea breeze. Any other cotton double knitting/ cotton 4 ply can be used provided the tension is the same.

	Body	Nightshirt/hat/shoes
pink flesh (268)	50 g	
nut brown (297)	oddments	
red (254)	oddments	
bleached (521)		25 g
blue polka (530)		25 g
oddments of yarn for features and candle		

Needles and notions

1 pair 4 mm (no. 8) needles; 1 bell; 2 small buttons; kapoc stuffing; ribbon for shoes

TENSION

24 sts. × 32 rows st.st. on 4 mm (no. 8) needles makes a 10 cm / 4 in square

PATTERN

(See also photograph on page 11.)

Body (make 2 pieces)
Start at lower edge. Using 4 mm (no. 8) needles and pink, cast on 12 sts.
Next row: (wrong side): purl.
Cont. in st.st., increasing 1 st. at each end on next 2 rows. *16 sts.*
Work 28 rows in st.st.
Dec. 1 st. at each end on next 2 rows.
Cast off.

Head (make 1 piece)
Using pink, cast on 8 sts.
1st row: (wrong side): purl.
Next row: * inc. in 1st st., rep. from * to end. *16 sts.*
Next row: purl.
Rep. last 2 rows. *32 sts.*
Work 20 rows in st.st.
Next row: * k2tog., rep. from * to end. *16 sts.*
Next row: purl.
Rep. last 2 rows. *8 sts.*
Cast off.

Arms (make 2 pieces)
Start at shoulder, using pink, cast on 2 sts.
1st row: (wrong side); purl.
Continuing in st.st, inc. 1 st. at each end on every row until 16 sts.
Next row: purl.
Work 20 rows in st.st.
Next row: * k2tog., rep. from * to end. *8 sts.*
Next row: purl.
Rep. the last 2 rows once. *4 sts.*
Break off yarn, leaving enough to thread through remaining sts. Draw up tightly and fasten off securely.

Feet and legs (make 2 pieces)
** Start at foot (1st side), using pink, cast on 8 sts.
1st row: (wrong side): purl.
Next row: k1, * inc. in next st., rep. from * to end. *15 sts.*
Next row: purl.
Work 5 rows in st.st.
Next row: p9, [p2tog.] 3 times. *12 sts.*
Next row: cast off 3 sts., k9 including st. on needle, slip sts. onto safety pin, do not break off yarn.
(2nd side) cast on 8 sts.
1st row: purl.
Next row: * inc. in next st., rep. from * to last st., k1. *15 sts.*
Next row: purl.
Work 5 rows in st.st.
Next row: [p2tog.] 3 times, p9. *12 sts.*
Next row: k9, cast off 3 sts. Fasten off.

Commence leg
Return to 1st side, purl 9 sts. from safety pin, p9 from 2nd side. **
Continue on these 18 sts.
Work 24 rows in st.st. Cast off.

Hat
Using 3¼ mm (no. 10) needles and blue, cast on 68 sts.

Starting with a knit row, work 3 rows in st.st.
Next row: knit to form a ridge.
Starting with a knit row, work 8 rows in st.st.
Next row: [k2tog., k13, k2tog. tbl] 4 times. *60 sts.*
Work 5 rows in st.st.
Next row: [k2tog., k11, k2tog. tbl] 4 times. *52 sts.*
Work 5 rows in st.st.
Continue to dec. in this way working 2 sts. less between decreases until 12 sts. remain.
Work 5 rows in st.st.
Next row: [k3tog.] 4 times. *4 sts.*
Break off yarn, leaving enough to thread through remaining sts. Draw up tightly and fasten off securely.

Shoes (make 2 pieces)
Using 3¼ mm (no. 10) needles and blue, cast on 17 sts. Work in garter st.
1st row: knit.
Next row: * inc. in next st., rep. from * to end. *34 sts.*
Knit 10 rows.
Next row: k8, turn, k2tog., knit to end.
Next row: k5, k2tog.
Knit 3 rows on these 6 sts. Cast off.
Rejoin yarn and work across centre 18 sts. as follows:
Next row: k2tog., k5, [k2tog.] twice, k5, k2tog., turn.
Next row: k2tog., k3, [k2tog.] twice, k3, k2tog.
Next row: [k2tog., k1, k2tog.] twice.
Cast off remaining 6 sts.
Rejoin yarn to remaining sts.
Next row: k2 tog., knit to end.
Next row: knit to last 2 sts., k2tog.
Knit 3 rows on these 6 sts.
Cast off.

Nightshirt
Patt. stripe: 2 rows cream, * 1 row blue, 1 row cream, rep. from * to end.
Using 3¼ mm (no. 10) needles, cast on 20 sts. Using st.st. and working patt., knit until work measures 14 cm / 5½ in.
Cast on 10 sts. Knit across. *20 sts.*
Cast on 10 sts. Knit across to end. *40 sts.*
Continue for 14 rows. Cast off.

Candle
Using 4 mm (no. 8) needles and red, cast on 4 sts.
Knit 6 rows in st.st. Cast off.

Make up
Join body by backstitching and stuff. Join arms, leaving 1st 8 rows open at shoulder, stuff and attach to body. Stitch thumb shape on hand. Join leg and feet seams, stuff and attach to body. Sew up seams of nightshirt, leaving opening for neck. Press. Sew 2 buttons on front neck and slip onto Wee Willie Winkie.
Join head, stuff and attach to body. Using brown yarn doubled, stitch large loops for hair. (Make a large loop with yarn, then secure, repeating all over head.) Join hat by backstitching, fold hem on wrong side and slipstitch into position. Sew onto head at back. Sew bell on end of hat.
For shoes, join back and foot seams by topstitching. Sew on ribbon and tie over instep. Embroider features on face: Swiss darn (see page 78) eyes; make a French knot for the nose and use back stitch for the mouth.
Sew up side and top seam of candle. Stuff and sew bottom up. Stitch onto Wee Willie Winkie's hand.

Hot Water Bottle Cover

MEASUREMENT

To fit a bottle 15 × 19 cm / 6 × 7½ in. A larger cover may be made by adding 6 more sts. for every 2.5 cm / 1 in in width.

MATERIALS

Wool

The numbers in brackets after the colours refer to Rowan Yarns cotton double knitting. Any other cotton double knitting can be used provided the tension is the same.

yellow (271)   50 g
pink flesh (268); bleached (521) *doubled*;   }
blue polka (530) *doubled*; nut brown (297) }   oddments
oddments of yarn for features

Alternative colourway
Use cherry red (298) in place of the yellow.

Needles

1 pair 4 mm (no. 8); crochet hook

TENSION

5½ sts. × 7½ rows st.st. on 4 mm (no. 8) needles makes a 2.5 cm / 1 in square

PATTERN (See also photograph on page 11.)

Using 4 mm (no. 8) needles and yellow, cast on 33 sts.
Following chart below:
1st row: knit.
2nd row: k1, purl to last st., k1.
Rep. these 2 rows until piece fits up to start of bottle neck, ending with 2nd row.
Next row: (make holes for cord): k1, * yf, k2tog., rep. from * to end.
Next row: k1, purl to last st., k1.
Work 6 rows in st.st. Cast off. Work embroidery and Swiss darning (see page 78).
Make another piece.

Make up
Stitch two pieces together. Make a crochet cord in blue (see page 78) and thread through holes, tie in bow at back.

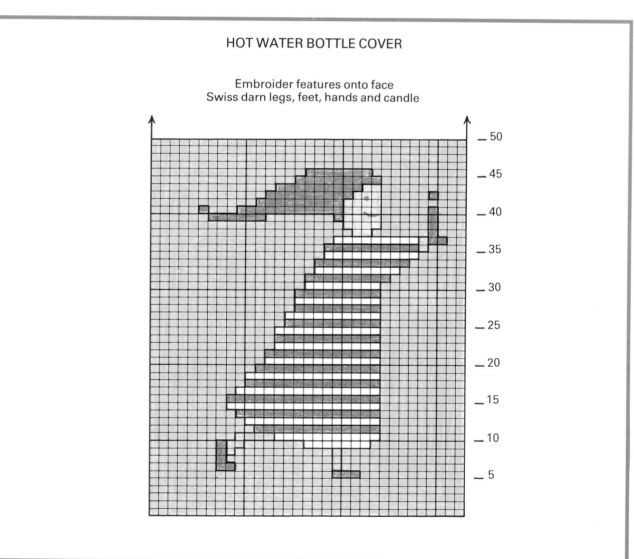

HOT WATER BOTTLE COVER

Embroider features onto face
Swiss darn legs, feet, hands and candle

Hickory, dickory, dock,
The mouse ran up the clock.
The clock struck one,
The mouse ran down,
Hickory, dickory, dock.

Hickory, Dickory, Dock

The clock the mouse ran up is featured on both ends of the long scarf accompanying this warm jumper for boys or girls. There's also a hat to keep the cold out. The busy little mouse is knitted into the pattern of the jumper but also appears as a detachable toy having a rest on the shoulder.

MEASUREMENTS

Jumper
Chest: 56 (61, 66) cm / 22 (24, 26) in
Sleeve: 24 (28, 31) cm / 9½ (11, 12¼) in

Hat (one size)
Width round head: 38 cm / 15 in

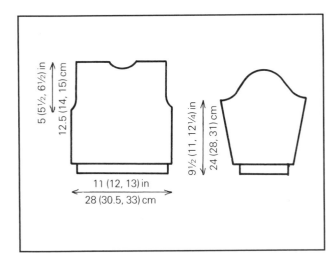

MATERIALS

Wool
The numbers in brackets after the colours refer to Rowan Designer and Flec double knitting. Any other double knitting can be used provided the tension is the same.

	Jumper	Scarf	Hat
flec (82F) [MS]	250 g (300 g, 350 g)	250 g	75 g
red (646)	25 g	use leftovers of colours	
blue (501)	25 g	use leftovers of colours	
yellow (648)	25 g	use leftovers of colours	
grey (61)	25 g		

Alternative colourway
A flecked black (62F) could be used in place of the flec as the main shade.

Needles and notions
1 pair 3¼ mm (no. 10) and 1 pair 4 mm (no. 8) needles; 8 decorative buttons; 2 large press studs (for detachable mouse); crochet hook

TENSION

22 sts. × 30 rows st.st. on 4 mm (no. 8) needles makes a 10 cm / 4 in square

PATTERN

JUMPER

Front
Using 3¼ mm (no. 10) needles and MS, cast on 73 (79, 85) sts.
Work 16 rows in k1, p1, rib.
Change to 4 mm (no. 8) needles.
Next row: knit, increasing 4 sts. evenly along row.
Cont. in st.st. following the chart on page 73, starting at row 1 and ending after row 64 (68, 76).

Shape armholes
Cast off 2 (3, 3) sts. at beg. of next 2 rows.

Dec. 1 st. at each end of needle on every row until 57 (61, 65) sts. remain.
Cont. without further dec. until armholes measure 8.5 (9, 10) cm / 3¼ (3½, 4) in, ending with a knit row.

Shape neck
Next row: p35 (p37, p40), slip the last 13 (13, 15) sts. just worked onto a stitch holder, purl to end.
Cont. on the last set of sts. as follows:
** Dec. 1 st. at neck edge on every row until 16 (16, 17) sts. remain.
Cont. without further dec. until armhole measures 12.5 (14, 15) cm / 5 (5½, 6) in, ending at armhole edge.

Shape shoulder
Cast off 5 sts. at beg. of next row, then 5 (5, 6) sts. at beg. of following alt. rows.
Work 1 row.
Cast off rem. 6 sts. **
With RS facing, rejoin yarn to rem. sts. at neck edge. Work as given for left side from ** to **.

Back
Work as for front to shape neck.
Cont. in st.st. until armholes measure same as front to shoulder, ending with a purl row.

Shape shoulders
Cast off 5 sts. at beg. of next 2 rows and 5 (5, 6) sts. at beg. of following 2 rows, then 6 sts. at beg. of next 2 rows.
Slip rem. 25 (29, 31) sts. onto a stitch holder.
Break off yarn.

Sleeves
Using 3¼ mm (no. 10) needles and MS, cast on 41 (43, 43) sts.
Work 16 rows in k1, p1, rib.
Change to 4 mm (no. 8) needles.
Cont. in st.st. increasing 1 st. at each end of the needle on the 5th and every following 6th (7th, 7th) row until 55 (59, 63) sts.
Cont. without further inc. until sleeve measures 24 (28, 31) cm / 9½ (11, 12¼) in from beginning, ending with a purl row.

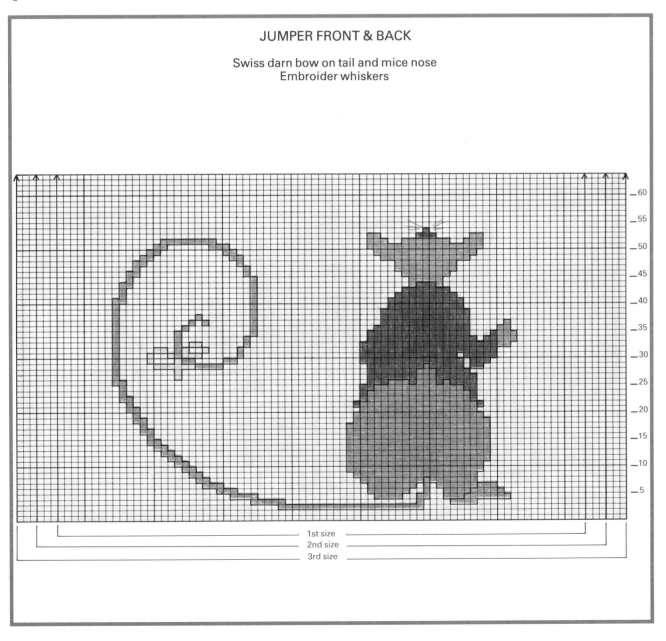

JUMPER FRONT & BACK

Swiss darn bow on tail and mice nose
Embroider whiskers

1st size
2nd size
3rd size

Shape top

Cast off 2 (3, 3) sts. at beg. of next 2 rows.
Dec 1 st. at each end of the needle on every row until 39 (41, 43) sts. remain.
Work 2 (2, 3) rows.
Dec. 1 st. at each end on the next and every following 4th row until 33 (33, 35) sts., then on every following alt. row until 25 sts. remain.
Work 1 row.
Cast off 3 sts. at beg. of next 4 rows.
Cast off rem. 13 sts.

Make up

Join right shoulder seam.

Neckband

With RS facing, using 3¼ mm (no. 10) needles and MS, pick up and knit 19 (21, 21) sts. down left side neck, knit 13 (13, 15) sts. from front neck stitch holder, pick up and knit 18 (20, 20) sts. up right side neck and knit 25 (29, 31) sts. from back neck stitch holder. *75 (83, 87) sts.*
Starting on a 2nd row, work 5 (5, 6) cm / 2 (2, 2½) in in k1, p1, rib.
Cast off loosely in rib.
Join left shoulder seam and join neckband. Fold neckband in half onto wrong side and slipstitch into position.
Join side seams and sleeve seams. Set in sleeves. Press.

Patches

Knit 2 patches each of 6 sts. × 6 rows worked in yellow and blue, alternating colours every 2 sts. and 2 rows for checked patt.
Sew patches onto front and back mice with cross st. using an oddment of contrasting coloured thread. Press. Swiss darn the mice noses and bows on tails. Work loop sts. for the whiskers, making sure they are attached firmly, then cut the loops. Sew 2 buttons on back of mice jackets on front and back of jumper. Sew 2 large press studs on top of sleeve to attach the toy mouse. To make this, follow the toy mouse pattern, halving everything.
This is optional, the mouse can be made simply as a toy if liked or it could be attached to the clock on the scarf.

SCARF

Using 3¼ mm (no. 10) needles and MS, cast on 73 sts.
Knit 1 row.
Cont. in st.st. for 4 rows, then follow the chart on page 75, starting at row 1 and still working in st.st.
Work 200 rows in st.st. in MS.
Follow the chart again, this time reversing it.
Work 5 rows in st.st.
Cast off.

Make up

Embroider hands and numbers on clock faces (see page 78). With right sides together, fold scarf in half lengthways. Join back seam, then turn right way out and press so that the seam is centre back of scarf.
To make fringes, cut yarn into 18 cm / 5 in lengths and taking 3 strands at a time, knot into both layers of the scarf at the short ends. Trim the fringes.

HAT

Using 3¼ mm (no. 10) needles, cast on 110 sts.
Work in k1, p1, rib until work measures 18 cm / 7 in.
Dec. 1 st. at beg. of last row. *109 sts.*

Shape crown

1st row: p2tog., * [k1, p1] 4 times, k1, sl.2, k1, psso, rep. from * to last 11 sts., [k1, p1] 4 times, k1, p2tog.
2nd row: [k1, p1] 5 times, * p2, [k1, p1] 4 times, rep. from * to last st., k1.
3rd row: [p1, k1] 5 times, * k2, [p1, k1] 4 times, rep. from * to last st., p1.
4th row: as 2nd row.
5th row: k2tog., * [p1, k1] 3 times, p1, sl.2, k1, psso, rep. from * to last 9 sts., [p1, k1] 3 times, p1, k2tog.
6th row: * p1, k1, rep. from * to last st., p1.
7th row: * k1, p1, rep. from * to last st., k1.
8th row: as 6th row.
9th row: p2tog., * [k1, p1] twice, k1, sl.2, k1, psso, rep. from * to last 7 sts., [k1, p1] twice, k1, p2tog.
10th row: [k1, p1] 3 times, * p2, [k1, p1] twice, rep. from * to last st., k1.
11th row: [p1, k1] 3 times, * k2, [p1, k1] twice, rep. from * to last st., p1.
12th row: as 10th row.
13th row: k2tog., * p1, k1, p1, sl.2, k1, psso, rep. from * to last 5 sts., p1, k1, p1, k2tog.
14th row: as 6th row.
15th row: p2tog., * k1, sl.2, k1, psso, rep. from * to last 3 sts., k1, p2tog.
16th row: p1, * p2tog., rep. from * to end.
Break off enough yarn to thread through remaining sts. Draw up tightly and fasten off securely.

Make up

Join seams, reversing seam for turn-up at lower edge. Make a pom-pom 5 cm / 2 in in diameter (see page 78) using all the bright colours. Attach to a crochet chain (see page 78) 7.5 cm / 3 in long and sew to top of hat. Stitch 2 mice buttons onto brim.

Toy Mouse

MEASUREMENTS

Height: approx. 15 cm / 6 in

MATERIALS

Wool

The numbers in brackets after the colours refer to Rowan Designer and Flec double knitting. Any other double knitting can be used provided the tension is the same.

grey (61)	25 g
red (646), blue (501), and yellow (648)	oddments

Needles and notions

1 pair 3¼ mm (no. 10) and 1 pair 4 mm (no. 8) needles; 1 × 4 mm (no. 8) crochet hook; kapoc stuffing; 3 buttons

TENSION

14 sts. × 18 rows st.st. on 3¼ mm (no. 10) needles makes a 5 cm / 2 in square
11 sts. × 14 rows st.st. on 4 mm (no. 8) needles makes a 5 cm / 2 in square

PATTERN

(See also photograph on page 11.)

BODY

Right leg

Using no 3¼ mm (no. 10) needles and blue, cast on 13 sts. for boots.
Next row: inc. once knitwise into every st. *26 sts.*
Starting with a purl row, work 7 rows in st.st. *

Shape top of foot
k3, [k2tog.] 8 times, k7. *18 sts.*
Next row: purl.
Next row: k2, [k2tog.] 5 times, k6. *13 sts.*
** Work 2 rows in st.st.
Work 2 rows in garter st.
Break off blue and work in red for trousers.
Work 2 rows in st.st. **
Leave these 13 sts. on a thread.

Left leg

Work as for right leg until *.
Shape top of foot
k7, [k2tog.] 8 times, k3. *18 sts.*
Next row: purl.
Next row: k6, [k2tog.] 5 times, k2. *13 sts.*
Work from ** to ** as given for right leg.

Body

Using red, knit across 13 sts. for left leg, pick up and knit 13 sts. left on thread for right leg. *26 sts.*
Next row: inc. once purlwise into every st. *52 sts.*
Work 6 rows.
Knit and slip 13 sts. onto thread, k26, slip rem. 13 sts. onto a thread.

Front

*** Working on these 26 sts., purl 1 row.
Cont. in st.st. for 10 rows.
Break off wool and join yellow. Work 4 rows.

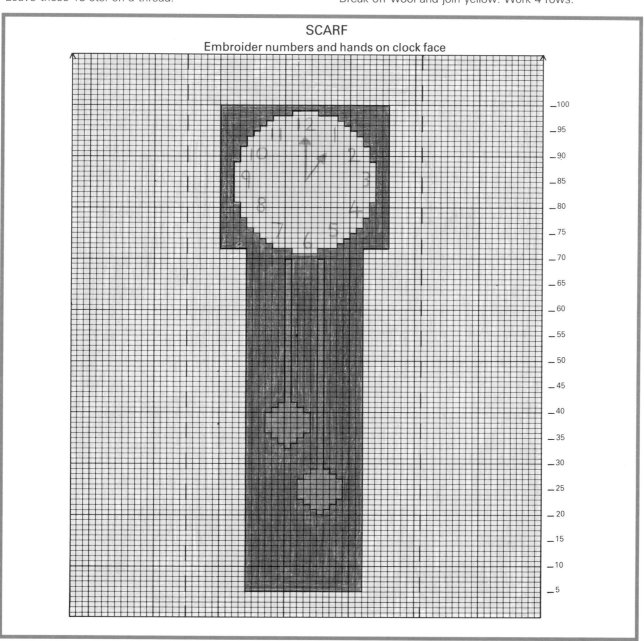

SCARF
Embroider numbers and hands on clock face

Dec. 1 st. at each end of next and every alt. row to 16 sts.
Work 1 row without shaping.
Leave these 16 sts. on a thread. ∗∗∗

Back

With right side facing and using red, start at side edge and pick up and knit 13 sts. left on thread for right leg, then pick up and knit 13 sts. left on thread for left leg. *26 sts.*
Work from, ∗∗∗ to ∗∗∗ as given for front.

Arms (make 2)

Using 3¼ mm (no. 10) needles and grey, cast on 7 sts.
Next row: inc. once knitwise into every st. *14 sts.*
Next row: purl.
Work 4 rows in st.st.
Next row: [k2tog.] 7 times. *7 sts.*
Break off MS and join yellow for shirt sleeves.
Next row: purl.
Next row: inc. once knitwise into every st. *14 sts.*
Next row: purl.

Shape arm

Working in st.st. as follows:
inc. 1 st. at each end of next and every alt. row until 18 sts.
Work 3 rows without shaping.

Shape top of arm

Dec. 1 st. at each end of next and every alt. row to 8 sts.
Work 1 row without shaping. Leave these 8 sts. on a thread.

Head

Using 3¼ mm (no. 10) needles and grey, cast on 7 sts.
Next row: inc. once knitwise into every st. *14 sts.*
Next row: purl.
Working in st.st. as follows:
inc. 1 st. at each end of every row until 28 sts.
Work 7 rows without shaping.
Next row: k4, k2tog., [k4, k2tog.] 3 times, k4. *24 sts.*
Work 3 rows without shaping.
Next row: k3, k2tog., [k2, k3tog.] 3 times, k4. *17 sts.*
Work 1 row without shaping.
Next row: k1, k2tog., [k1, k3tog.] 3 times, k2. *10 sts.*
Work 1 row without shaping.
Break off enough yarn to thread through rem. 10 sts. Draw up tightly and fasten off securely.

Ears (make 2)

Using 3¼ mm (no. 10) needles and grey, cast on 10 sts.
Next row: inc. once knitwise into every st. *20 sts.*
Next row: purl.
Work 8 rows in st.st.
Next row: [k2tog.] 10 times. *10 sts.*
Next row: purl.
Next row: [k2tog.] 5 times. *5 sts.*
Break off enough yarn to thread through rem. 5 sts. Draw up tightly and fasten off securely.

Tail

Using a 4 mm (no. 8) crochet hook, make a crochet chain (see page 78) 15 cm / 6 in long.

Make up

Sew up foot and leg seams. Sew up raglan seams. Sew up body seam. Sew up arm seams. Stuff body and arms. Run yarn through sts. left on threads at top of body and arms and fasten off. Sew up head seam leaving opening for stuffing. Stuff and sew up.
Sew head onto body. Fold ears in half and sew up seams. Sew ears onto head. Sew on tail. Embroider features. Knit a patch as for the jumper (see page 74) and stitch onto trousers with cross st.

Coat (in one piece to armholes)

Using 4 mm (no. 8) needles and blue, cast on 44 sts.
Work 2 rows in garter st.
Next row: knit and slip 2 sts. onto a thread, k 40, slip rem. 2 sts. onto a thread.
Next row: purl.
Cont. in st.st. until work measures 3 cm / 1¼ in, ending with a knit row.
Next row: (divide for armhole): p9, cast off 2 sts., p19, cast off 2 sts., p8.

Left front

∗∗ Working on these 9 sts. cont. until work measures 5.5 cm / 2¼ in, ending with a purl row.

Shape neck

Dec. 1 st. at neck edge in every row to 6 sts.
Work 1 row without shaping.
Cast off. ∗∗

Back

Rejoin yarn to next 19 sts. and cont. in st.st. until work measures same as left front. Cast off.

Right front

Rejoin yarn to rem. 9 sts. and work from ∗∗ to ∗∗ as given for left front.
Sew up shoulder seams.

Sleeves (make 2)

Using 4 mm (no. 8) needles and blue, cast on 13 sts.
Work 2 rows in garter st.
Working in st.st., inc. 1 st. at each end of next and every alt. row until 19 sts.
Work 1 row without shaping. Cast off.
Sew up sleeve seams and sew onto coat.

Collar

With wrong side facing, using 4 mm (no. 8) needles and blue, pick up and knit 6 sts. up right side of neck, 10 sts. across back of neck and 6 sts. down left side of neck. *22 sts.*
Work 5 rows in garter st.
Cast off.

Borders

Using 3¼ mm (no. 10) needles and blue, pick up 2 sts. left on thread and inc. to 4 sts.
Work in garter st. until border measures 5.5 cm / 2¼ in. Cast off.
Repeat other side.
Sew button in middle and make a chain loop buttonhole to match.

Pockets

Using 4 mm (no. 8) needles and blue, cast on 5 sts.
Work 4 rows in st.st., then 2 rows in garter st. Cast off.
Sew onto front of coat. Sew 2 buttons onto back of coat.
To attach mouse to sweater, sew 1 large press stud onto front body and 1 to neck to correspond with ones on shoulder of jumper.

Order numbers from the Button Box (see next page) for the buttons used are as follows:

This little piggy: pink pigs – NP60
Hey diddle, diddle: brown cows – HP26–C
Hickory, dickory, dock: brown mice – NP40
        red cherries – NP45
        coloured hearts – N6
Little Bo-peep: white lambs – HP25–A
        black lamb – HP25–B
Little Jack Horner: yellow clock – HP23–A

Sing a song of sixpence: musical notes (small) – NP10
        (large) – NP6 & NP7
Wee Willie Winkie: blue squirrels – HP36–A & hearts as above
Humpty Dumpty: strawberries – HP44
        purple & red hands – N22
Ring-a-ring o' Roses: pink & lilac flowers – PX38
Ladybird, ladybird: red ladybirds – HP12

Techniques

SWISS DARNING

This is worked on stocking stitch. The embroidery repeats the design of the original stitch. Use a yarn of the same thickness as the knitting, so that the knitted stitches are fully covered.
1. Bring the needle from the back of the work to the front in the middle of the stitch below the one to be covered. Hold the free end of the yarn at the back of the work (diagram 1).
2. Pass the needle under the two strands of the stitch above and bring it back to the starting point. Pass it under the two strands of the stitch on the left (diagram 2).
3. Work this stitch as before following step 2. Work in the same way across the first row of the motif. To work a second row, turn work and begin the next row still working from right to left (diagram 3). Darn in the free end.

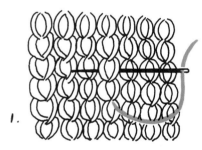

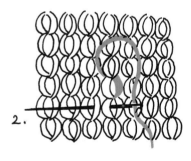

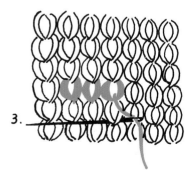

FRENCH KNOTS

Bring the needle up through to the front of the knitting and wind the yarn twice round the needle (diagram 1). Insert needle back through knitting at the same point as it entered and pull the yarn tight to form a knot (diagram 2). Fasten off.

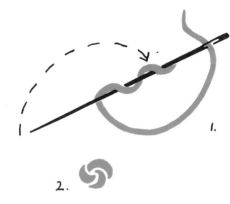

DAISY STITCH

Work a single stitch as shown in diagrams 1 and 2 to make a chain stitch. Put these together in groups of four to form a petal (diagram 3).

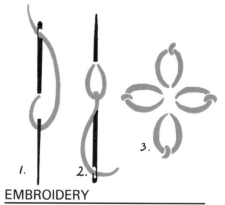

EMBROIDERY

Use embroidery for features too small to knot or to Swiss darn. For example use running stitch for the outline of eyes and fill in with over stitch. Use over stitch for the mouth with a running stitch at either end and running stitch for nose and eyebrows. Embroidery can be mixed with Swiss darning.

TASSELS

Wind the yarn round four fingers until it is the required thickness. Cut off the yarn and wind the end round the loops just made several times to bind them together 2 cm / ½ inch from one end. Fasten securely. Cut the loops at the bottom.

CROCHET CHAIN CORD

Start by making a slip loop several inches from the end of the yarn and slip this onto the crochet hook. This loop counts as the first chain. Catch the yarn with the hook and pull it through the loop already on the hook (see diagram). Continue making stitches in this way until the cord is the length required. Pull the yarn completely through the last stitch to fasten off.

POM-POMS

1. Cut 2 circles of card to required diameter and make a 1 cm (½ inch) hole in the centre of each (diagram 1).
2. Place these two circles together. Thread a needle with yarn used double and wind round card circles covering all the card until the central hole is full (diagram 2).
3. Using a sharp pair of scissors, cut round the outer edge of the circles between the two cards (diagram 3).
4. Tie a length of yarn very tightly round the centre between the two cards and fasten tightly. Remove the cards and clip any uneven ends (diagram 4).

KNITTING WITH A CHANGE OF COLOUR

Weaving method
Use this method to deal with the yarn not being used if more than 3 stitches of a contrast colour are being knitted. It avoids having large loops of wool hanging at the back of the knitting. The background yarn (the one not being knitted) is woven on the wrong side of the work.
1. Pass the contrast yarn over the forefinger of the right hand and the background yarn over the forefinger of the left hand. On a knit row, pass the right hand needle once under the background yarn (diagram 1) and once over it (diagram 2) before working the next stitch. Always keep the background yarn on the wrong side of the knitting.
2. On a purl row, work the same way keeping the yarn at the front of the work (wrong side of knitting). Pass the right hand needle once under (diagram 3) and once over (diagram 4) the background yarn before working the next stitch.

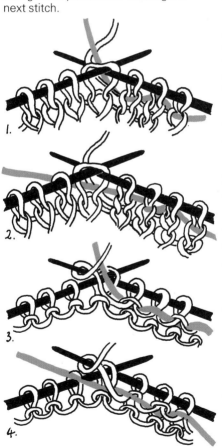

Winding method
This method is to be used if large areas are being worked in a contrast colour. Use separate balls of yarn for each colour and do not carry the yarn along the back of the work. At each colour change, cross the yarns on the wrong side of the work to avoid holes in the knitting. The yarn from the last stitch must pass over the yarn to be used for the next stitch (diagrams 1 and 2).

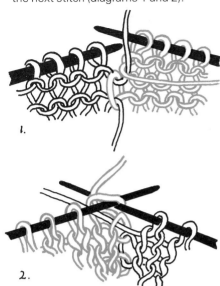

WORKING FROM CHARTS

One square on the charts represents one stitch. The charts are mainly followed for colour sequences but watch for separate instructions in the captions. Work surface embroidery when the piece is finished.

SEWING UP

To sew up the clothes and the toys, use either a running stitch or an over stitch. Use the same colour of yarn as the pieces being joined. Gently press the seams when finished.

ADAPTING THE MEASUREMENTS

To increase or decrease the length of a pattern, first check the tension to find how many rows there are per centimetre or inch. Multiply this number by the number of centimetres or inches you wish to add or subtract. Make this adjustment on a straight piece of knitting.

CARE OF GARMENTS

Hand wash articles knitted in pure wool carefully in soap flakes. Squeeze gently and give a short spin. Do not leave wet. Ease back into shape and dry flat. For wool mixtures, check manufacturer's instructions on label.
Hand wash cotton knitting carefully. Squeeze dry and ease back into shape. Dry flat.

STOCKISTS

Rowan Yarns
The author and publisher wish to thank Rowan Yarns, Green Lane Mill, Holmfirth, West Yorkshire, England, for supplying the yarns for the patterns in this book.
Rowan Yarns are available throughout the U.K. and at the following stockists overseas:

USA
The Westminster Trading Corporation,
5 Northern Boulevard,
Amherst,
New Hampshire 03031

CANADA
Estelle Designs and Sales Ltd,
38 Continental Place,
Scarborough,
Ontario, M1R 2T4

AUSTRALIA
Sunspun Enterprises Pty Ltd,
195 Canterbury Road,
Canterbury,
3126 Victoria

NEW ZEALAND
Creative Fashion Centre,
PO Box 45083,
Epuni Railway,
Lower Hutt

HOLLAND
Henk and Henrietta Beukers,
Dorpsstraat 9,
5327 AR Hurwenen

NORWAY
Eureka,
Kvakkestandgarden,
1400 Ski

SWEDEN
Wincent,
Luntmakargatan 56,
113 58 Stockholm

Button Box
The author and publisher also wish to thank the Button Box for supplying all the buttons (see page 77).
The buttons are available by mail order from Button Box, P.O. Box 289, London, WC2E 9SG or from the shop: Button Box, 44 Bedford Street, Covent Garden, London WC2E 9HA, England

Bells, squeakers and kapoc stuffing
These are available from specialist craft shops and craft departments in large stores.

Notes

ABBREVIATIONS

k	knit
p	purl
st. (s.)	stitch (es)
st.st.	stocking stitch (one row knit, one row purl)
g. st.	garter stitch (every row knit)
sl.1	slip one stitch (transfer one stitch from left needle, knitwise unless otherwise stated, to right hand needle)
sl.1(k)	slip one stitch knitwise
sl.1(p)	slip one stitch purlwise
m1	make one stitch (pick up horizontal loop lying before next stitch and work into the back of it)
m1(k)	make one stitch knitwise
m1(p)	make one stitch purlwise
inc.	increase (ing)
dec.	decrease (ing)
incs	increases
decs	decreases
yf	yarn forward
yb	yarn back
yrn	yarn round needle
tbl	through back of loop
psso	pass slipped stitch over
beg.	begin (ning)
rem.	remain (ing)
rep.	repeat
alt.	alternate
tog.	together
cont.	continue (ing)
patt.	pattern
foll.	following
mm	millimetre (s)
cm	centimetre (s)
in	inch (es)
MS	main shade
RS	right side
WS	wrong side
*	repeat directions following the asterisks as indicated
[ ]	repeat directions inside brackets as many times as indicated

U.S.A. GLOSSARY

cast off	bind off
tension	gauge
stocking stitch	stockinette stitch
work straight	work even
yarn forward	
yarn round needle	yarn over
Swiss darning	duplicate stitch
4 ply yarn	lightweight
double knitting yarn	knitting worsted
chunky yarn	bulky yarn

MEASUREMENTS

The **chest** measurement is the actual chest size of the child taken round the chest, under the arms.

Page 79 gives information on adapting a pattern to the measurements of your child.

YARN QUANTITIES

Quantities for the yarn used are given with each pattern in metric quantities. To calculate how many ounces of yarn are needed, divide the grams by 28.4 and round up to the nearest whole number.

SIZE NOTE

The instructions are given for the smallest size, the one or two larger sizes are given in brackets.

SIZE CHART

Age	6 mths–1 yr	1–2 yrs	2–3 yrs	3–4 yrs	4–5 yrs
cm	46	51	56	61	66
in	18	20	22	24	26

NEEDLE CHART

Metric	9 mm	7½ mm	7 mm	6½ mm	6 mm	5½ mm	5 mm	4½ mm	4 mm	3¾ mm	3¼ mm	3 mm	2¾ mm
English	00	1	2	3	4	5	6	7	8	9	10	11	12
American	13	11	–	10½	10	9	8	7	6	5	4	–	2